Writing Strategies That Work

Learn the 10 keys to effective writing instruction! In this dynamic book, best-selling author Lori G. Wilfong takes you through today's best practices for teaching writing and how to implement them in the classroom. She also points out practices that should be avoided, helping you figure out how to update your teaching so that all students can reach success.

You'll discover how to . . .

- ♦ Make sure students have enough work in a genre before you assign writing
- ♦ Develop thoughtful, short writing prompts that are "infinite" and not finite
- ♦ Have students read and learn from master authors in the genre in which they are writing
- ♦ Create a writing community so that writing is not an isolated activity
- ♦ Use anchor charts and minilessons, along with rubrics and checklists
- ♦ Implement revising strategies, not just editing strategies, taught in context
- ♦ Use conferencing to grow students as thoughtful, reflective writers
- ♦ Let narratives be personal and creative, focusing on details and imagery
- ♦ Let informational writing explore a topic creatively and in depth
- ♦ Let argument writing be situated in real-world application and not be limited to one-sided, "what-if" debates

Every chapter begins with an engaging scenario, includes the "why" behind the practice and how it connects to the Common Core, and clearly describes how to implement the strategy. The book also contains tons of handy templates that you can reproduce and use in your own classroom. You can photocopy these templates or download them from our website at www.routledge.com/books/details/9781138812444.

Lori G. Wilfong is a former middle school language arts teacher, current Associate Professor in Middle Childhood Education at Kent State University, frequent conference presenter, and forever supporter of teachers working to weave literacy into their classrooms.

Writing Strategies That Work

Do This—Not That!

Lori G. Wilfong

Routledge
Taylor & Francis Group

NEW YORK AND LONDON

First published 2015
by Routledge
711 Third Avenue, New York, NY 10017

and by Routledge
2 Park Square, Milton Park, Abingdon, Oxon, OX14 4RN

Routledge is an imprint of the Taylor & Francis Group, an informa business

Library of Congress Cataloging-in-Publication Data

Wilfong, Lori G.
    Writing strategies that work : do this, not that / by Lori G. Wilfong.
        pages cm
    Includes bibliographical references.
    1. Creative writing (Elementary education)   I. Title.
    LB1576.W4876575 2015
    372.62'3—dc23
    2014046338

ISBN: 978-1-138-81243-7 (hbk)
ISBN: 978-1-138-81244-4 (pbk)
ISBN: 978-1-315-74881-8 (ebk)

Typeset in Palatino
by Apex CoVantage, LLC

For Ms. Brayer, Mr. Friedenberg, and Mr. Lowe—three teachers who always made me feel like a writer. Thank you for making the classroom a magical place.

Contents

Setup of This Book

To describe each item on the **Do This—Not That** list, this text has been set up with a specific structure:

♦ A description of the research behind each "Do This" item

♦ Strategies that update traditional instructional practice for each item on the list

♦ Common Core State Standards that correlate with each strategy

♦ Action steps and reflection items for each item to help spur your instructional change!

eResources

The templates featured in this book are also available as free eResources on our website, at www.routledge.com/books/details/9781138812444. Click on the tab that says eResources. Teachers can print and photocopy these tools for classroom use.

Meet the Author

Lori G. Wilfong, PhD, began her career as a naïve (and yet know-it-all) teacher at a middle school in East Los Angeles. Two days into her job teaching English to sixth-, seventh-, and eighth-grade English Language Learners, she realized how much she didn't know about teaching, and this set the course for the rest of her career: to learn as much as she could about motivating adolescent readers, reading in the content areas, young adult literature, and differentiated instruction. A frenzy of advanced degree getting followed, including a master's in Reading Specialization and a doctorate in Curriculum & Instruction, both from Kent State University. She worked as a literacy coach and a literacy specialist in rural and urban districts in Northeast Ohio before landing in the department of Teaching, Learning, and Curriculum Studies at Kent State University at Stark, Ohio, where she currently is an Associate Professor, teaching courses in literacy to both preservice and practicing teachers.

Lori continues to hone her skills in school districts, working with teachers with one goal always in mind: to make all students love reading. She previously authored *Vocabulary Strategies That Work: Do This—Not That!*, published in late 2012, and *Nonfiction Strategies That Work: Do This—Not That!*, published in spring 2014. She lives in Munroe Falls, Ohio, with her husband, Bob.

DO THIS!	NOT THAT . . .
1. Let writing come from a place of writing, taking students through the three types of writing necessary for building a Common Core Writers' Workshop	1. Assign writing without previous work in the genre
2. Develop thoughtful, short writing prompts that are "infinite," not finite	2. Only give writing prompts that can be answered in brief sentences or paragraphs without elaboration
3. Have students read, critique, and learn from master authors in the genre they are writing	3. Have students write without exposing them to readings from the genre
4. Create a writing community in your classroom	4. Have writing be an isolated, individual activity in your classroom
5. Use anchor charts and minilessons to explicitly teach writing	5. Only give rubrics or checklists to show what is required in a piece of writing
6. Emphasize content and revision when helping students develop as writers, teaching editing in the context of student writing	6. Skip or limit revising strategies in favor of isolated editing drills while only emphasizing mechanics while grading
7. Use conferencing to grow students as thoughtful, reflective writers	7. Use conferencing to edit or correct papers, with a scattered focus.
8. Let narratives be personal and creative, focusing on details and imagery to make a story come to life	8. Limit narrative writing to "One time . . ." stories
9. Let informational writing explore a topic creatively	9. Limit informational writing to shallow exploration of a topic
10. Let argument writing be situated in real-world application	10. Limit argument writing to one-sided, "what-if" debates

Take a look at your writing teaching practices, and based on the list, record the following:

Things I am doing now that need to be updated:	Instructional updates I can use:

Brainstorm: What evidence can you provide to show that you are changing your instructional practice in the teaching of writing?

_____

_____

_____

_____

_____

_____

_____

_____

_____

_____

_____

_____

_____

_____

_____

_____

_____

Introduction

What more is there to say about writing? After doing the research for this book, I wasn't sure if there was really more to say about the topic—so much has already been said! But after talking with teachers from all over the country, it seemed that writing was on the mind of every teacher as they realized the importance that was placed on writing in the Common Core State Standards. It wasn't like writing wasn't being taught—it was!—but very few teachers seemed satisfied with their instruction. That was when the new "do this—not that" list started to take shape: There were a lot of practices happening in writing instruction that seemed outdated that needed updating, and the resulting list turned into this book, *Writing Strategies That Work: Do This—Not That!*

"Do this—not that!" sums up my philosophy of professional development. As a teacher, professor, and consultant, I found that the instruction I received and later delivered centered on telling teachers what were the best practices in education. This seemed right until I returned to my own classroom and felt completely overwhelmed—what strategies should I get rid of? What strategies should I keep? And what usually happened? I went back to teaching the exact same way I always did. That is why this book is set up to tell you what practices have become outdated that you can discard and what teaching practices you can implement instead.

Enjoy the practice of updating your writing practices!

Chapter 1

Let Writing Come From a Place of Writing, Taking Students Through the Three Types of Writing Necessary for Building a Common Core Writers' Workshop

My colleague Sarah came into my classroom at the end of the school day, a stack of papers in her arms. "This is hopeless," she sighed, thumping the stack on my desk. I picked the top one up. "What are these?" I asked, skimming the black-ink, blue-lined page. "Character analysis in The Outsiders. They are awful. And I don't get why. I gave them two weeks to write the paper. We took notes while we read the book. We did an outline. I corrected rough drafts. There really wasn't anything else I could do to make these better, short of writing the papers for them."

Why Is This Item on the List So Important?

As a seventh grade teacher, Sarah had certain expectations of her students. She felt that they should come to her primed to write. Her scaffolds of taking notes, creating an outline, and correcting rough drafts felt like teaching to her. But when I asked her what craft lessons she had taught about the kind of writing she wanted students to produce, she looked confused. "Didn't I say we did an outline?"

This anecdote perfectly illustrates doing writing *to* students: After reading, students were given an assignment and expected to instinctively know what was appropriate for that genre. Teaching writing came in the form of outlines, which can be a helpful beginning tool when brainstorming, and editing, a last stop in the writing process. But there was nothing to bridge this gap between the two, and both the students and Sarah were frustrated.

This writing scenario plays out in classrooms everywhere. It is what makes the teaching of writing such a sticky, messy, WONDERFUL process that is scary for teachers to tackle. In a recent professional development on writing I conducted, I polled the teachers about which language arts process they felt most proficient teaching: reading or writing. Out of 56 teachers, only three raised their hands for writing.

> Do this—not that principle #1: DO let writing come from a place of writing, taking students through the three types of writing necessary for building a Common Core Writers' Workshop. DON'T assign writing without previous work in the genre.

To Get Started

Writers' Workshop is not a new idea. In fact, the moment you read those words, Writers' Workshop, a certain fear may have entered your heart from what you think you *do* know about it. Many teachers think Writers' Workshop and think traditional elementary teaching practices: Loads of unfinished pieces with no real due dates, chaotic classrooms with students in various stages of writing without direction, haphazard grades, no attention to grammar, spelling, or punctuation, and narratives, narratives, and more narratives (did I say narratives?).

Let's myth-bust a bit when it comes to Writers' Workshop. Teaching in a workshop can be broken down like this: A focus skill or idea is introduced, modeled, and guided by the teacher. Students are then given time to practice the idea or skill on their own, with material that is of interest to them. Conferencing to ensure correct application of the focus skill or idea is conducted by the teacher in place of arbitrary workbook or worksheet pages.

There are other tenets of Writers' Workshop that are central to this philosophy of teaching:

1. A Writers' Workshop systematically scaffolds and teaches each genre of writing, as dictated by the *Common Core State Standards: Narrative, Informative Expository, and Opinion/Argument* (CCSS, 2010). Expectations exist for a student to produce work within each genre, with choice and guidance in the various formats that make up that type of writing.

2. A Writers' Workshop recognizes the sophistication that each grade level is asked to add to each writer by the three core writing standards, and teaches these through minilessons to ensure that students understand exactly what is required to make a great piece of writing.

3. A Writers' Workshop attends to the five parts of the writing process: Brainstorming, Drafting, Revising, Editing, and Publication.

4. A Writers' Workshop provides time in class (as much as possible!) for students to apply minilessons to their own writing.

5. A Writers' Workshop asks that the teachers write with and in front of students, blurring the roles of master and apprentice in a teaching workshop.

6. A Writers' Workshop meets students where they are as writers and moves them forward (Calkins, 1986).

Framing a Writers' Workshop in a 4–12 ELA Classroom

With these tenets in mind, I began to flesh out what it meant to run a Writers' Workshop in today's classroom, especially for intermediate, middle, and high school teachers. In my dream world, every teacher would have 45 minutes (or more!) to run a true Writers' Workshop. But the reality for the majority of teachers I work with is harsh; most tell me they have 50-minute class sessions to squeeze in all the goodness that Language Arts has to offer. These are the tenets that I add to the earlier ones, based on what I know teachers need to be successful in today's classroom:

1. Time in the classroom should depend on the emphasis of the instruction: reading or writing. Deliberately focusing on a type of ELA instruction allows the teacher to be purposeful and intentional when working through a unit.

2. Choice is given to students within a genre to ensure that the student voice is honored while the standard is still taught.

3. Clear deadlines are necessary to ensure appropriate pacing through the three genres.

The three instructional updates in this chapter are the three types of writing that make up a modern, middle childhood/adolescent–appropriate Writers' Workshop. Together, these form the basis for a unit; two basic templates for unit planning are shared at the end of the chapter (one for block teaching and one for single period instruction), incorporating these three types of writing!

Before you continue, think about your year in terms of pacing. If you were to sequence the three main genres of writing in your classroom over three quarters of instruction, what would you start with? There is no recommendation on what is best (although I find that most teachers seem to sequence the three genres of writing as narrative, informative, and argument), but have a sequence in mind as you learn about the types of writing required in each unit.

Instructional Practices to Update

Updated Strategy #1: Using Everyday Writing to Warm Up Students in the Focus Genre

As every athlete knows, a warm-up is necessary. Without it, injury could be imminent. And coupled with warm-up is practice, that essential time for athletes at every level to hone their craft, whether it is dribbling the ball down the court in a carefully designed drill or running wind sprints to increase speed for a game.

Everyday writing (or quickwrites, prompts, journaling—whatever you want to call it) is a warm-up coupled with practice. I am hoping you are saying to yourself, "I do this!" right now . . . because I know you do. But to bring a Common Core sensibility to everyday writing, a tighter focus needs to be brought to the classroom:

♦ *Everyday writing within a unit needs to focus on one genre for the majority of the time.* For example, if you have designated the first 9 weeks of your year as a narrative unit, then the majority of your everyday writing prompts need to address narrative writing (creating great prompts within a specific genre is addressed in chapter 2). This gives students the "warm-up" necessary to stretch out a bit within the genre.

♦ *Everyday writing needs to happen for an extended number of days.* I find that the rule of thumb is that a student needs to try out writing in a genre at least five times before they find a piece that actually merits finishing. This gives students the opportunity to abandon writing to a prompt that didn't "speak" to them.

♦ *Everyday writing is not an entire period of instruction.* In fact, in a school where teachers are pressed for time, everyday writing should happen during the Reading Emphasis of the 50-Minute Period Unit Planner at the end of the chapter (if you have a block, see the Block Writing Unit Planner). If you are reading amazing narratives, you can have students trying their hand at their own narratives during everyday writing. I actually have a very specific amount of time that a student should write during everyday writing: 7 minutes and 42 seconds. This is very scientific (I hope the sarcasm came across there). Five minutes for writing is too short, and ten minutes is too long. And 7 minutes and 42 seconds is hard for a student to figure out on an analog clock (so they are not clock-watching). This number was created by the National Writing Project at Kent State University by Teacher Consultant (and now Assistant Professor at Miami of Ohio) Kathy Batchelor, and I swear by it.

♦ *Sharing of everyday writing is brief.* I have seen teachers turn everyday writing into an all-day thing by letting students share their writing one-by-one around the classroom. While I am thrilled that students want to share their writing, we know we have to keep moving. I let students share with an elbow buddy (someone sitting next them) or at their tables. Sharing is brief and timed to keep us on track. If time allows, I ask students to "point nominate" an everyday writing they thought was exceptionally brilliant to share with the whole class (as a former middle school teacher, I find that kids will rarely nominate their own writing for sharing but their partners are always willing to "point nominate" a friend!).

♦ *Teachers should write along with their students during everyday writing.* Just as you should read when students are independently reading (Atwell, 2014), you need to write during everyday writing (Gallagher, 2011; Kittle, 2008). This could be privately, in your own writer's notebook, or publicly, on an overhead, truly in front of your students. Either way, by writing during the everyday writing period, you are beginning to build the models that you will need during Guided Writing to teach authentic minilessons.

You may have noticed a term I used earlier, the Reading Emphasis. I find that teachers with 50 minutes or less of daily instruction simply cannot do justice to both reading and writing instruction. To combat this, I designated instructional weeks as either the Reading Emphasis or the Writing Emphasis.

Table 1.1 Everyday Writing Rubric

3	2	1
Student fully responds to the prompt given creatively and expressively.	Student may wander off topic from the prompt.	Student does not address the prompt.

During the Reading Emphasis, the writing that is taking place is either Everyday Writing or writing in response to reading. During the Writing Emphasis, reading instruction takes a back seat while Guided Writing (and its accompanying mentor texts, chapter 3!) takes the wheel.

Grading. Always at this juncture in a professional development session on this topic, teachers begin to itch in their seats a bit. I asked a squirmer what the issue was: "Lori, I have to have grades for writing and you are telling me that for one to three weeks, students are just journaling? How do I grade that?" In Wilfong's Wonderful Writing World (an amusement park that I am going to build where ideal writing conditions exist), everyday writing would not be for a grade. But in reality, I understand that teachers feel pressure to put grades into their online grade books that are often viewed by parents on a nightly basis. During the everyday writing phase, I encourage teachers to look at everyday writing weekly, reading perhaps one entry from the week to check for adherence to the prompt. If necessary, don't tell students which prompt you will be reading (so they will be more inclined to work on all of them instead of just the one you will be using for a grade). But you can tell students to dog-ear what they think is their best writing of the week, a great beginning step in using reflection during the writing process. I urge teachers to resist the yearning to edit everyday writing—this is not the time! Breaking out your red pen at this juncture is a dream-squasher and does not get at the purpose of everyday writing. Simply let the ideas speak and let the rest go. Table 1.1 is a sample everyday writing rubric that a teacher could use for grading during this section of everyday writing.

Updated Strategy #2: Using Guided Writing to Bring an Everyday Writing Piece to Fruition

After so many writing prompts, it is time to switch to a Writing Emphasis in ELA instruction. I begin this period of instruction by holding a Draft Day (a name bestowed on this day by a very enthusiastic Cleveland Browns fan, because this is a day that holds so much promise for people who live in my area). Students are invited to read through all of their everyday writing pieces and pick (aka draft!) one they want to finish. They are then given time in class to complete this draft—a day or two, depending on what you know about your students. This happens without instruction from me. They are simply told to finish a piece they started during everyday writing.

We now get to the heart of Writers' Workshop: guided writing. Guided writing is where the magic happens in instruction. I usually start guided writing with a statement like this:

> Now that you have completed a full draft, we are going to spend the next few weeks making that piece of writing better. Every day, I am going to show you something you can use to strengthen that draft.

Students' automatic response to this statement is usually, "But I'm done!" Guided writing combats the reluctance to return to a draft; through choice, ownership, and carefully crafted lessons, students are led through the process of focusing on a single strategy to apply to their paper. This idea is born from Ralph Fletcher, who eloquently stated, "Writing needs to come from a place of writing" (2003). Students are more likely to return to a draft if I am showing them focused changes to make to their writing, one at a time, rather than throwing a checklist or rubric at them.

Before guided writing begins, I study the standard that guides the teaching of this particular genre and narrow down the standard to the specific elements that distinguish it from the other two. Figure 1.1 demonstrates this

Figure 1.1 Standards-Based Argument Writing Elements for Guided Writing

W 6.1 Write arguments to support claims with clear reasons and relevant evidence.
a. *Introduce claim(s)* and *organize the reasons and evidence clearly.*
b. *Support claim(s) with clear reasons and relevant evidence, using credible sources* and demonstrating an understanding of the topic or text.
c. *Use words, phrases, and clauses to clarify the relationships among claim(s) and reasons.*
d. Establish and *maintain a formal style.*
e. *Provide a concluding statement or section* that follows from the argument presented.
CCSS, 2010

process. Italicized in this figure are the elements that I need to teach during guided writing in a sixth grade class that is focusing on the argument genre.

Using the standard, I identified seven possible revision minilessons for guided writing:

1. Introduce claim(s) (W6.1a).
2. Organize the reasons and evidence clearly (W6.1a).
3. Support claim(s) with clear reasons and relevant evidence (W6.1b).
4. Use credible sources (W6.1b).
5. Use words, phrases, and clauses to clarify the relationship among claim(s) and reasons (W6.1c).
6. Maintain a formal style (W6.1d).
7. Provide a concluding statement or section (W6.1e).

This provides a perfect roadmap to follow when designing the revision lesson sequence for instruction during argumentative writing.

I next go to the Language Standards to identify the editing standards necessary for polishing a piece of writing in this genre. Figure 1.2 shows my thought process for choosing these minilessons.

Figure 1.2 Standards-Based Language Elements for Guided Writing

L 6.1 Demonstrate command of the conventions of standard English grammar and usage when writing or speaking.
a. *Ensure that pronouns are in the proper case* (subjective, objective, possessive).
b. *Use intensive pronouns* (e.g., *myself, ourselves*).
c. *Recognize and correct inappropriate shifts in pronoun number and person.*
d. *Recognize and correct vague pronouns* (i.e., ones with unclear or ambiguous antecedents).
e. Recognize variations from standard English in their own and others' writing and speaking, and identify and use strategies to improve expression in conventional language.
L 6.2 Demonstrate command of the conventions of standard English capitalization, punctuation, and spelling when writing.
a. Use punctuation (commas, parentheses, dashes) to set off nonrestrictive/parenthetical elements.

b. Spell correctly.
L 6.3 Use knowledge of language and its conventions when writing, speaking, reading, or listening.
a. Vary sentence patterns for meaning, reader/ listener interest, and style.
b. *Maintain consistency in style and tone.*
<div align="right">CCSS, 2010</div>

The good news with the Language standards is that all of them do NOT have to be taught during a single genre. Instead, I like to consider the Language standards in light of the genre being taught; which ones lend themselves best to the type of writing we are studying? To continue this unit on argumentative writing at sixth grade, I chose only two specific language minilessons:

1. Recognize, use, and correct intensive pronoun use, shifts in pronouns, and vague pronouns (combining L6.1 a, b, c, and d).
2. Maintain consistency in style and tone.

Depending on the ability of my writers, I may also include editing minilessons on other grammar elements: punctuation, capitalization, and so forth.

I keep throwing this word around, minilesson. Chapter 5 is all about crafting strategic, artful minilessons and the anchor charts that support them, so I don't want to say too much here. But a minilesson is a short (20 minutes or less) gradual release of responsibility where students are explicitly shown exactly how to apply an element of the genre to their writing through modeling, guided practice, and eventually independent practice (Bento, 2012; Fountas & Pinnell, 2000). Students should leave a minilesson with an action plan to make their writing better.

Here is an important tip to keep in mind as you complete a template at the end of this chapter with your minilesson sequence: Some teachers have the time to teach a minilesson and have students apply the concept on the same day. Other teachers like to move more slowly teaching a minilesson on one day and giving the next day over to application and conferencing. This depends on the pace you are setting and the time you have in your writing period. Both templates are available for you to play around with as you move forward!

Grading. After the minilesson sequence in both revision and editing has been taught, allow students a short amount of time to polish a final draft. Once this draft is submitted, it becomes a summative grade, one that is graded against a rubric based on the standards-based minilessons taught. But grades

Table 1.2 Minilesson Application Rubric

3	2	1	0
Student demonstrates a clear understanding of the element of the genre in their writing.	Student is progressing toward capable use of the element of the genre in their writing.	Student is learning to use the element of the genre in their writing.	Student is not applying the element of the genre in their writing.

can also come during the guided writing period itself; as students are applying the minilessons to their drafts, checks can be done for proper application, alerting the teacher to reteaching opportunities. These checks can be done during independent practice of the minilessons taught or on application days. The issue with this is that you will rarely get to conference with every student after every minilesson. If you can wait to take a grade until after you have conferenced with every student, great. If you need a grade sooner, have students highlight or underline the application of the minilesson in their writing for you so that you can simply flip through their notebook, look at these changes, and give points as needed. This can be a great opportunity for differentiation, too; the application of the minilesson can be scaffolded to the level of the writer. Take sensory language: Imagine you have just taught a minilesson on sensory language. Because you know your students' writing abilities from the pre-unit on-demand assessment (explained in the next section of this chapter), you know which students struggle with sensory language and which excel. Rather than giving the generic directive to put sensory language into student narratives, you can customize the application by setting goals for individual students. A proficient student can be asked to add sensory language to specific targets, such as setting and characters. A struggling student can be given a specific number of instances of sensory language to use. A rubric for guided writing minilesson application is provided in Table 1.2.

Updated Strategy #3: Using an On-Demand Assessment to Strategically Choose Minilessons and Document Growth in Writers

In *Pathways to the Common Core*, Calkins, Ehrensworth, and Lehman (2012) lay out the need for the on-demand assessment component of writing instruction: During Writers' Workshop, we are scaffolding every step of the way through minilessons to help students create fabulous final drafts, inclusive of

Table 1.3 Partial Student Evidence Rubric–Narrative (sixth grade)

NARRATIVE EXPECTATIONS (Grade 6)	PRE Self-Assessment * Scale of 1 to 4	EVIDENCE	PRE Teacher Assessment	EVIDENCE	POST Self-Assessment	EVIDENCE	POST Teacher Assessment	EVIDENCE
Write narratives to develop real or imagined experiences or events using effective technique, relevant descriptive details, and well-structure event sequences.								
Engage and orient the reader by establishing a context and introducing a narrator and/or characters. (a)								
Organize an event sequence that unfolds naturally and logically. (a)								

all the elements of that genre of writing. Graded against a standards-based rubric, these final drafts should be in pretty good shape. But how do students perform when those scaffolds are removed? That is where the on-demand assessment comes in—it is the place where you, the teacher, get to see if your instruction took hold in each student.

In true backward design fashion (Wiggins & McTighe, 2005), it is advisable to come up with your on-demand writing prompt and rubric prior to the unit being taught. Using the method from Figures 1.1 and 1.2, identify the minilessons you will teach and let those be the "meets" level of a standards-based rubric. Then, come up with two prompts for students to write to: one for before the unit and one for after the unit. Make these your best prompts, both engaging and focusing on the genre of study for the unit.

Administer one prompt before the unit even starts. This allows you to get a baseline on student writing in this genre. A colleague of mine made a student evidence-based rubric to capture this pre-/post-unit assessment: After students do the pre-unit assessment, allow them to view the rubric and provide evidence from their own writing of whether they are meeting a standard. They can then set goals for their growth as a writer over the course of this unit, and you can use the data to inform which minilessons might get be skipped (or added!), based on student proficiency. Table 1.3 provides a sample of a standards-based Student Evidence Rubric, with space for both the student and the teacher to look for evidence in the student's writing of elements of the genre.

Grading. Two grades can be taken from the on-demand assessment (just as important, though, is the fact that no grade should be taken from the pre-unit on-demand assessment). One grade is a summative grade on the post-unit on-demand assessment, a measure of how a student can apply the elements of the genre in a non-scaffolded setting. The second grade is a growth grade—allow students to view their writing from both the pre-unit on-demand assessment and the post. How have they grown as a writer? Did they meet the goal that they set after the pre-unit on-demand assessment? This kind of reflection can result in great conversation and metacognition.

Common Core Connection

All of the writing standards connect well with the content covered in this chapter (see Table 1.4).

Table 1.4 Writing Standards Addressed in This Chapter

Grade Level	4	5	6
Standard Addressed	**Writing** Write opinion pieces on topics or texts, supporting a point of view with reasons and information. Introduce a topic or text clearly, state an opinion, and create an organizational structure in which related ideas are grouped to support the writer's purpose. b. Provide reasons that are supported by facts and details. c. Link opinion and reasons using words and phrases (e.g., *for instance, in order to, in addition*). d. Provide a concluding statement or section related to the opinion presented. Write informative/	**Writing** Write opinion pieces on topics or texts, supporting a point of view with reasons and information. Introduce a topic or text clearly, state an opinion, and create an organizational structure in which ideas are logically grouped to support the writer's purpose. Provide logically ordered reasons that are supported by facts and details. Link opinion and reasons using words, phrases, and clauses (e.g., *consequently, specifically*). Provide a concluding statement or section related to the opinion presented. Write informative/	**Writing** Write arguments to support claims with clear reasons and relevant evidence. Introduce claim(s) and organize the reasons and evidence clearly. Support claim(s) with clear reasons and relevant evidence, using credible sources and demonstrating an understanding of the topic or text. Use words, phrases, and clauses to clarify the relationships among claim(s) and reasons. Establish and maintain a formal style. Provide a concluding statement or section that follows from the argument presented. Write informative/

(Continued)

Table 1.4 Continued

Grade Level	4	5	6
	explanatory texts to examine a topic and convey ideas and information clearly. a. Introduce a topic clearly and group related information in paragraphs and sections; include formatting (e.g., headings), illustrations, and multimedia when useful to aiding comprehension. b. Develop the topic with facts, definitions, concrete details, quotations, or other information and examples related to the topic. c. Link ideas within categories of information using words and phrases (e.g., *another, for example, also, because*). d. Use precise language and domain-specific	explanatory texts to examine a topic and convey ideas and information clearly. Introduce a topic clearly, provide a general observation and focus, and group related information logically; include formatting (e.g., headings), illustrations, and multimedia when useful to aiding comprehension. Develop the topic with facts, definitions, concrete details, quotations, or other information and examples related to the topic. Link ideas within and across categories of information using words, phrases, and clauses (e.g., *in contrast, especially*). Use precise language and domain-specific	explanatory texts to examine a topic and convey ideas, concepts, and information through the selection, organization, and analysis of relevant content. Introduce a topic; organize ideas, concepts, and information, using strategies such as definition, classification, comparison/ contrast, and cause/effect; include formatting (e.g., headings), graphics (e.g., charts, tables), and multimedia when useful to aiding comprehension. Develop the topic with relevant facts, definitions, concrete details, quotations, or other information and examples. Use appropriate transitions to clarify the relationships among ideas and concepts.

Grade Level	4	5	6
	vocabulary to inform about or explain the topic. e. Provide a concluding statement or section related to the information or explanation presented. Write narratives to develop real or imagined experiences or events using effective technique, descriptive details, and clear event sequences. Orient the reader by establishing a situation and introducing a narrator and/or characters; organize an event sequence that unfolds naturally. Use dialogue and description to develop experiences and events or show the responses of characters to situations.	vocabulary to inform about or explain the topic. Provide a concluding statement or section related to the information or explanation presented. Write narratives to develop real or imagined experiences or events using effective technique, descriptive details, and clear event sequences. Orient the reader by establishing a situation and introducing a narrator and/or characters; organize an event sequence that unfolds naturally. Use narrative techniques, such as dialogue, description, and pacing, to develop experiences and events or show	Use precise language and domain-specific vocabulary to inform about or explain the topic. Establish and maintain a formal style. Provide a concluding statement or section that follows from the information or explanation presented. Write narratives to develop real or imagined experiences or events using effective technique, relevant descriptive details, and well-structured event sequences. Engage and orient the reader by establishing a context and introducing a narrator and/or characters; organize an event sequence that unfolds naturally and logically.

(*Continued*)

Table 1.4 Continued

Grade Level	4	5	6
	Use a variety of transitional words and phrases to manage the sequence of events. Use concrete words and phrases and sensory details to convey experiences and events precisely. Provide a conclusion that follows from the narrated experiences or events. Write routinely over extended time frames (time for research, reflection, and revision) and shorter time frames (a single sitting or a day or two) for a range of discipline-specific tasks, purposes, and audiences.	the responses of characters to situations. Use a variety of transitional words, phrases, and clauses to manage the sequence of events. Use concrete words and phrases and sensory details to convey experiences and events precisely. Provide a conclusion that follows from the narrated experiences or events. Write routinely over extended time frames (time for research, reflection, and revision) and shorter time frames (a single sitting or a day or two) for a range of discipline-specific tasks, purposes, and audiences.	Use narrative techniques, such as dialogue, pacing, and description, to develop experiences, events, and/or characters. Use a variety of transition words, phrases, and clauses to convey sequence and signal shifts from one time frame or setting to another. Use precise words and phrases, relevant descriptive details, and sensory language to convey experiences and events. Provide a conclusion that follows from the narrated experiences or events. Write routinely over extended time frames (time for research, reflection, and revision) and shorter time frames (a single

Grade Level	4	5	6
			sitting or a day or two) for a range of discipline-specific tasks, purposes, and audiences.

	7	8	9–10
	Writing Write arguments to support claims with clear reasons and relevant evidence. Introduce claim(s), acknowledge alternate or opposing claims, and organize the reasons and evidence logically. Support claim(s) with logical reasoning and relevant evidence, using accurate, credible sources and demonstrating an understanding of the topic or text. Use words, phrases, and clauses to create cohesion and clarify the relationships among claim(s),	**Writing** Write arguments to support claims with clear reasons and relevant evidence. Introduce claim(s), acknowledge and distinguish the claim(s) from alternate or opposing claims, and organize the reasons and evidence logically. Support claim(s) with logical reasoning and relevant evidence, using accurate, credible sources and demonstrating an understanding of the topic or text. Use words, phrases, and clauses to create cohesion and clarify the	**Writing** Write arguments to support claims in an analysis of substantive topics or texts, using valid reasoning and relevant and sufficient evidence. Introduce precise claim(s), distinguish the claim(s) from alternate or opposing claims, and create an organization that establishes clear relationships among claim(s), counterclaims, reasons, and evidence. Develop claim(s) and counterclaims fairly, supplying evidence for each while pointing out the strengths and limitations of

(Continued)

Table 1.4 Continued

	7	8	9–10
	reasons, and evidence. Establish and maintain a formal style. Provide a concluding statement or section that follows from and supports the argument presented. Write informative/ explanatory texts to examine a topic and convey ideas, concepts, and information through the selection, organization, and analysis of relevant content. Introduce a topic clearly, previewing what is to follow; organize ideas, concepts, and information, using strategies such as definition, classification, comparison/ contrast, and cause/	relationships among claim(s), counterclaims, reasons, and evidence. Establish and maintain a formal style. Provide a concluding statement or section that follows from and supports the argument presented. Write informative/ explanatory texts to examine a topic and convey ideas, concepts, and information through the selection, organization, and analysis of relevant content. Introduce a topic clearly, previewing what is to follow; organize ideas, concepts, and information into broader categories; include formatting	both in a manner that anticipates the audience's knowledge level and concerns. Use words, phrases, and clauses to link the major sections of the text, create cohesion, and clarify the relationships between claim(s) and reasons, between reasons and evidence, and between claim(s) and counterclaims. Establish and maintain a formal style and objective tone while attending to the norms and conventions of the discipline in which they are writing. Provide a concluding statement or section that follows from and supports the argument presented.

	7	8	9–10
	effect; include formatting (e.g., headings), graphics (e.g., charts, tables), and multimedia when useful to aiding comprehension. Develop the topic with relevant facts, definitions, concrete details, quotations, or other information and examples. Use appropriate transitions to create cohesion and clarify the relationships among ideas and concepts. Use precise language and domain-specific vocabulary to inform about or explain the topic. Establish and maintain a formal style. Provide a concluding statement or section that follows from	(e.g., headings), graphics (e.g., charts, tables), and multimedia when useful to aiding comprehension. Develop the topic with relevant, well-chosen facts, definitions, concrete details, quotations, or other information and examples. Use appropriate and varied transitions to create cohesion and clarify the relationships among ideas and concepts. Use precise language and domain-specific vocabulary to inform about or explain the topic. Establish and maintain a formal style. Provide a concluding statement or section that follows from and supports	Write informative/ explanatory texts to examine and convey complex ideas, concepts, and information clearly and accurately through the effective selection, organization, and analysis of content. Introduce a topic; organize complex ideas, concepts, and information to make important connections and distinctions; include formatting (e.g., headings), graphics (e.g., figures, tables), and multimedia when useful to aiding comprehension. Develop the topic with well-chosen, relevant, and sufficient facts, extended definitions, concrete details,

(Continued)

Table 1.4 Continued

	7	8	9–10
	and supports the information or explanation presented. Write narratives to develop real or imagined experiences or events using effective technique, relevant descriptive details, and well-structured event sequences. a. Engage and orient the reader by establishing a context and point of view and introducing a narrator and/ or characters; organize an event sequence that unfolds naturally and logically. b. Use narrative techniques, such as dialogue, pacing, and description, to develop experiences, events, and/or characters.	the information or explanation presented. Write narratives to develop real or imagined experiences or events using effective technique, relevant descriptive details, and well-structured event sequences. a. Engage and orient the reader by establishing a context and point of view and introducing a narrator and/or characters; organize an event sequence that unfolds naturally and logically. b. Use narrative techniques, such as dialogue, pacing, description, and reflection, to develop experiences, events, and/or characters.	quotations, or other information and examples appropriate to the audience's knowledge of the topic. Use appropriate and varied transitions to link the major sections of the text, create cohesion, and clarify the relationships among complex ideas and concepts. Use precise language and domain-specific vocabulary to manage the complexity of the topic. Establish and maintain a formal style and objective tone while attending to the norms and conventions of the discipline in which they are writing. Provide a concluding statement or section that

	7	8	9–10
	c. Use a variety of transition words, phrases, and clauses to convey sequence and signal shifts from one time frame or setting to another. d. Use precise words and phrases, relevant descriptive details, and sensory language to capture the action and convey experiences and events. e. Provide a conclusion that follows from and reflects on the narrated experiences or events. Write routinely over extended time frames (time for research, reflection, and revision) and shorter time frames (a single sitting or a day or two) for a range of discipline-specific tasks, purposes, and audiences.	c. Use a variety of transition words, phrases, and clauses to convey sequence, signal shifts from one time frame or setting to another, and show the relationships among experiences and events. d. Use precise words and phrases, relevant descriptive details, and sensory language to capture the action and convey experiences and events. e. Provide a conclusion that follows from and reflects on the narrated experiences or events. Write routinely over extended time frames (time for research, reflection, and revision) and shorter time frames (a single sitting or a day or two) for a range	follows from and supports the information or explanation presented (e.g., articulating implications or the significance of the topic). Write narratives to develop real or imagined experiences or events using effective technique, well-chosen details, and well-structured event sequences. Engage and orient the reader by setting out a problem, situation, or observation, establishing one or multiple point(s) of view, and introducing a narrator and/or characters; create a smooth progression of experiences or events. Use narrative techniques, such as dialogue, pacing, description,

(Continued)

Table 1.4 Continued

		7	8	9–10
			of discipline-specific tasks, purposes, and audiences.	reflection, and multiple plot lines, to develop experiences, events, and/or characters. Use a variety of techniques to sequence events so that they build on one another to create a coherent whole. Use precise words and phrases, telling details, and sensory language to convey a vivid picture of the experiences, events, setting, and/or characters. Provide a conclusion that follows from and reflects on what is experienced, observed, or resolved over the course of the narrative. Write routinely over extended time frames (time for research, reflection, and revision) and shorter time

	7	8	9–10
			frames (a single sitting or a day or two) for a range of tasks, purposes, and audiences.

Action Steps

A Common Core Writers' Workshop is within your reach! It is time to take some action . . .

1. On which genre of writing (from informational, narrative, or argument) are you planning to center your unit?

    _____

2. Start with the end in mind. What are two great writing prompts within your genre? List these here, for use in a pre- and post-unit on-demand assessment.

    a. _____

    _____

    b. _____

    _____

3. What are five everyday writing prompts that meet that genre? List them here:

    a. _____

    _____

    b. _____

    _____

    c. _____

    _____

    d. _____

    _____

    e. _____

    _____

4. Now, take a look at the writing standards for your grade level (make sure you pay attention to the *letters* under the anchor standard). List the minilessons necessary to meet the elements of this genre, based on the standard. Remember, a single standard may be broken down into multiple minilessons!

a. _____

_____

b. _____

_____

c. _____

_____

d. _____

_____

e. _____

_____

f. _____

_____

g. _____

_____

h. _____

_____

5. What language standards are a good match for this genre? What other language standards do you know that your students need more work on (punctuation, spelling, etc.)? List the language minilessons you want to teach with this genre.

a. _____

_____

b. _____

_____

c. _____

_____

d. _____

_____

5. Consider one of the unit planning templates included at the end of this chapter. Take the unit components you created in numbers one through five and fill out the unit planner. You are on your way!

Works Cited

Atwell, N. (2014). *In the middle, third edition: A lifetime of learning about writing, reading and adolescents*. Portsmouth, NH: Heinemann.

Bento, S. (2012). Scaffolding: An ongoing process to support adolescent writing instruction. *Journal of Adolescent and Adult Literacy, 56*, 291–300.

Calkins, L. (1986). *The art of teaching writing*. Portsmouth, NH: Heinemann.

Calkins, L., Ehrensworth, M., & Lehman, C. (2012). *Pathways to the Common Core: Accelerating achievement*. Portsmouth, NH: Heinemann.

Fletcher, R. (2003). *A writer's notebook: Unlocking the writer within you*. New York: HarperCollins.

Fountas, I., & Pinnell, G. (2000). *Guiding readers and writers (grades 3–6): Teaching comprehension, genre and content literacy*. Portsmouth, NH: Heinemann.

Gallagher, Kelly. (2011). *Write like this: Teaching real-world writing through modeling and mentor texts*. Portland, ME: Stenhouse.

Kittle, P. (2008). *Write beside them: Risk, voice, and clarity in high school writing*. Portsmouth, NH: Heinemann.

National Governors Association Center for Best Practices & Council of Chief State School Officers. (2010). *Common Core State Standards for English language arts and literacy in history/social studies, science, and technical subjects*. Washington, DC: Authors.

Wiggins, G., & McTighe, J. (2005). *Understanding by design*. Alexandria, VA: ASCD.

Template 1.1 Unit Planner (50-minute periods)

This unit planner allows for teachers to continue to do both reading and writing within the short instructional time because of the minilessons on one day and time to apply the minilesson on a separate day.

Focus	Monday	Tuesday	Wednesday	Thursday	Friday
On-demand assessment/ everyday writing	Pre-unit on-demand writing assessment:	Everyday writing prompt #1:		Everyday writing prompt #2:	
Everyday writing	Everyday writing prompt #3:		Everyday writing prompt #4:		
Everyday writing/ draft day/ begin guided writing	Everyday writing prompt #5:	Draft day (students choose one of their prompts to take to completion)	Drafting Day (students complete their drafts)	Minilesson #1:	Application/ conferencing day
Guided writing	Minilesson #2:	Application/ conferencing day	Minilesson #3:	Application/ conferencing day	Catch-up day
Guided writing	Minilesson #4:	Application/ conferencing day	Minilesson #5:	Application/ conferencing day	Catch-up day
Guided writing	Minilesson #6:	Application/ conferencing day	Minilesson #7:	Application/ conferencing day	Catch-up day
Guided writing	Minilesson #8:	Application/ conferencing day	Minilesson #9:	Application/ conferencing day	Catch-up day
Post-unit on-demand assessment	Polishing the final draft	Polishing the final draft	Writing celebration!		Post-unit on-demand assessment

Template 1.2   Reading/Writing Emphasis Unit Planner (50-minute periods)

This unit planner allows teachers to emphasize either reading or writing instruction over the course of a traditional, 9-week quarter. Minilessons and application/conferencing occur on the same time, since the entire 50 minutes is devoted to guided writing on these days.

Focus	Monday	Tuesday	Wednesday	Thursday	Friday
On-demand assessment/ Everyday writing *Reading Emphasis*	Pre-unit on-demand writing assessment:	Everyday writing prompt #1:		Everyday writing prompt #2:	
Everyday writing *Reading Emphasis*	Everyday writing prompt #3:		Everyday writing prompt #4:		
Everyday writing *Reading Emphasis*	Everyday writing prompt #5:		Everyday writing prompt #6:		
Everyday writing *Reading Emphasis*	Everyday writing prompt #7:		Everyday writing prompt #8:		
Everyday writing *Transition to Writing Emphasis*	Everyday writing prompt #9:		Everyday writing prompt #10:	Draft day (students choose one of their prompts to take to completion)	Drafting day (students complete their drafts)
Guided writing *Writing Emphasis*	Minilesson #1:	Minilesson #2:	Minilesson #3:	Minilesson #4:	Catch-up day
Guided writing *Writing Emphasis*	Minilesson #5:	Minilesson #6:	Minilesson #7:	Minilesson #8:	Catch-up day
Post-unit on-demand assessment *Writing Emphasis*	Minilesson #9:	Polishing the final draft	Polishing the final draft	Writing celebration!	Post-unit on-demand assessment

© 2015, *Writing Strategies That Work,* Lori G. Wilfong, Routledge

Template 1.3 Block Unit Planner

Lucky you! You can do a full Writers' Workshop, allowing time to continue your excellent reading practices while devoting 45 minutes daily to writing instruction. A few extra tidbits are here that will be explained in later chapters: writing territories, regular writing sharing, and more!

Focus	Monday	Tuesday	Wednesday	Thursday	Friday
On-demand assessment/ Everyday writing	Pre-unit on-demand writing assessment:	Genre writing territory	Everyday writing prompt #1:	Everyday writing prompt #2:	Writing group meeting
Everyday writing	Everyday writing prompt #3:	Everyday writing prompt #4:	Everyday writing prompt #5:	Everyday writing prompt #6	Writing group meeting
Everyday writing/ Draft day/ Begin guided writing	Everyday writing prompt #7:	Draft day (students choose one of their prompts to take to completion)	Drafting day (students complete their drafts)	Writing group meeting	Minilesson #1: application/ conferencing
Guided writing	Minilesson #1 reminder: application/ conferencing	Minilesson #2	Minilesson #2 reminder: application/ conferencing	Writing group meeting	Catch-up day
Guided writing	Minilesson #3: application/ conferencing	Minilesson #3 reminder: application/ conferencing	Minilesson #4: application/ conferencing	Minilesson #4 reminder: application/ conferencing	Writing group meeting
Guided writing	Minilesson #5: application/ conferencing	Minilesson #5 reminder: application/ conferencing	Minilesson #6: application/ conferencing	Minilesson #6 reminder: application/ conferencing	Writing group meeting
Guided writing	Minilesson #7: application/ conferencing	Minilesson #7 reminder: application/ conferencing	Minilesson #8: application/ conferencing	Minilesson #8 reminder: application/ conferencing	Writing group meeting
Post-unit on-demand assessment	Minilesson #9: application/ conferencing	Polishing the final draft	Polishing the final draft	Writing celebration!	Post-unit on-demand assessment

Chapter 2

Develop Thoughtful, Short Writing Prompts That Are "Infinite," Not Finite

I set the timer for seven minutes and students bent their heads over their notebooks to respond to the prompt on the board. After 90 seconds, most heads were lifted back up (or lying flat on desks, preparing for a nap). I walked over to the nearest student and peeked at his work. The prompt was, "What is your favorite day of the week and why?" He had written, "I like Saturday because I get to sleep in." I whispered to him, "Don't you have any more to say about that?" He gave me a withering look. "No. I'm done."

Why Is This Item on the List So Important?

"I'm done." Those may be two of the most disliked words by teachers working on writing with students. "I'm done" implies finality—and a student's extreme reluctance to return to their work to add something, let alone revise or edit. Preventing "I'm done" is at the heart of a writing workshop; it is that magic moment when the timer goes off and students are still writing furiously because they have so much to say.

On the surface, the premise of a writing prompt seems simple—you post the prompt, you give the students a set amount of time to respond, and you move on with life—maybe sharing responses, maybe using these as the springboard for bigger writing assignments. But the thinking behind the prompt needs to be more than "respond to this"—to avoid the "I'm done" syndrome, the prompt itself becomes of paramount importance.

Walt Disney once said that a blank page is the most exciting entity in the world to him—it held the infinite promise of the ideas that could be spilled upon it. It is this infinite promise that leads us to our second principle.

> **Do this–not that principle #2: DO develop thoughtful, short writing prompts that are "infinite," not finite. DON'T give only writing prompts that can be answered in brief sentences or paragraphs without elaboration.**

To Get Started

Simply defined, a writing prompt is anything that prompts a student to write. Traditionally, they are divided into a few categories:

♦ **Questions**—These are the predominant prompts out there. Students write in response to a question, such as, "What is your favorite day of the week and why?" presented in the anecdote at the beginning of the chapter.

♦ **Thought-provokes**—I coined this term to cover the categories of quotes, videos, and songs that teachers present to students to spark writing.

♦ **Story Starters**—Usually ending with an ellipses, these prompts give students an idea to run with, in the vein of, "*It was a dark and stormy night . . .*"

Writing prompts are used for more than keeping students quiet for the first 10 minutes of class (or bell work). As an initial writing activity, they help students wrangle the complexity of facing a blank page by giving them a focus (Carroll & Feng, 2010). In content area classes, writing prompts help teachers address the content through writing (Furtak & Ruiz-Primo, 2008). As assessments, writing prompts give students the lead-in necessary to be successful in "on-demand" writings that demonstrate fluency, content, and communication skills (Calkins, 2010).

Olinghouse, Zheng, and Morlock (2012) identified six characteristics of motivating tasks and prompts for writers:

1. Time allocation—Students are given plenty of time to respond to a prompt with writing.

2. Audience specification—The recipient of the writing is clarified through the task.

3. Audience intimacy—Students know their intended audience well.

4. Definition of task—Students understand the prompt and/or type of writing it demands.

5. Allowance for multiple perspectives—Students have the ability to interpret the prompt in multiple ways.

6. Real-world relevance and purpose—The prompt addresses topics and issues that students find interesting and relatable.

Using these six characteristics is a good way to initially vet writing prompts that you use in your classroom. My earlier prompt falls flat in audience specification, audience intimacy, definition of task, and real-world relevance. I gave them an appropriate amount of time for response (time allocation), and it could be interpreted a number of ways (allowance for multiple perspectives), but these two elements of good prompts were not enough to keep my students writing or interested in stretching their responses.

Occasionally, I have gotten pushback from teachers on characteristic #6, from Olinghouse et al. (2012). A teacher recently stated to me during a professional development workshop, "They can't get to write about what they like all the time, especially on tests. They need to learn to respond to uninteresting prompts, too." I tend to agree—not every prompt you write, whether for bell work, minilesson application, or assessment, is going to speak to every student. But if we write prompts that fit the other five characteristics of motivating tasks and prompts, we will have made it easier for them to be successful!

Instructional Strategies to Update

Updated Strategy #1: Identifying Finite Versus Infinite Prompts to Use at Appropriate Times in Instruction

Coming up with or identifying good prompts is not easy. I found this out firsthand during the Summer Institute of the National Writing Project at Kent

State University. A group of teachers and I were sitting around a table, discussing the difficulties of getting students to participate in initial writing, when it occurred to me that the problem was not *the students* (whom it is easy to blame), but more *the prompts* that we give students to respond to. I asked the teachers to list a few of their favorite prompts on the whiteboard at the front of the room for group analysis. Staring at the prompts, which ranged from simple response questions to in-depth analysis of great works of literature, it became clear that the prompts fell into one of two categories: infinite or finite (Table 2.1).

To illustrate the finite/infinite writing prompt principle, Table 2.2 shows several sample prompts that fall into each category.

Table 2.1   Infinite Versus Finite Writing Prompts

Infinite Prompts	Finite Prompts
They can be answered in multiple ways.	The response is straightforward (think factual—social studies or science).
It is hard for a student to say, "I'm done," after writing for a few minutes because there is always more that could be added.	They can easily be answered in a few sentences.
They might be more than just a traditional question (pictures, songs, quotes).	Depth or explanation is not necessary or required to provide an appropriate response to the prompt.

Table 2.2   Sample Infinite and Finite Writing Prompts

Infinite Writing Prompts	Finite Writing Prompts
Who is thankful for you? Tell a story that illustrates why this person feels this way (a twist on the usual Thanksgiving quote).	Name five events that led to the beginning of the Revolutionary War.
Is global warming a real or perceived phenomenon? Prepare an argument that looks at both sides of the issue. Be prepared to choose and defend a side.	What do you want to be when you grow up and why?
Play the song "Springsteen" by Eric Church for the class (you may wish to have the lyrics printed out for students to read along with).	Give one example from the past week of how you used math in your everyday life.

The infinite prompts in Table 2.2 are shown for a reason—they make students squirm a bit. I have never seen students more uncomfortable than when asked to identify someone who was thankful for *them*. Students got to work, but it took a few minutes of thinking (and questioning me) before they bent their heads over their notebooks.

The global warming prompt illustrates a type of prompt all its own—controversy. Many students have specific opinions on specific topics, and this prompt was used as the kickoff for an argument paper in a high school science classroom. Even the students without a lot of background on the topic had something to say; this prompt became the basis for an extended piece of writing that involved research and debate.

The final infinite prompt, the song, is the most "out of the box" example. I did not pose a question to the students after I played the song. I simply set the timer (this was an everyday writing assignment) for 8 minutes and said, "Go for it." A few students stared at me, and one raised his hand to ask, "What do you want me to write now?" My response was, "Whatever you feel inspired to write." More stares followed that response, but in the end, we heard stories about songs that students had chosen as special with a particular loved one, a response detailing the power of music, and even one diatribe about how much one student disliked country music. Now THAT was infinite—a song evoked so many different responses, each personal and unique!

Infinite prompts take some getting used to. When I began using these with preservice teachers this past fall, the first few weeks of Grounds for Thought (the writing time that started every class session—name credited to the National Writing Project at Kent State University!) had many questions that mirror the earlier student response—"What do you want here?" After a few weeks, students got that I wasn't looking for a "right" answer—I was looking for their response, whatever that may be!

The finite prompts most likely look and feel more comfortable to both you as a teacher and to students. Expectations are clear; "name five" or "give one" helps clarify exactly what students are supposed to do, while responding to questions in writing is something students have been doing since they began kindergarten!

When do I use each type of prompt? Both infinite and finite prompts have a place in all classrooms. By employing this principle, you are being very purposeful in the task you set forth for students.

Infinite prompts: These types of prompts are great for everyday writing/bell work scenarios in language arts classes as a way to get brains working. In content area classes, infinite prompts can lead to argument or informative papers about a topic that will be explored in depth. In all classes, infinite prompts can become great lead-ins for more extended writing experiences or to give students a chance to try out a specific genre or authorial technique.

Finite prompts: These types of prompts lend themselves well to formative and summative assessment, times when you need to see if the students are grasping the concepts you have taught. Entrance slips, exit slips, the "think" in think-pair-share—all of these are tailored for finite prompts.

Updated Strategy #2: Using RAFT to Help Students Clarify Their Audience and Define the Task in Writing

Even when faced with the greatest prompt in the world, many students struggle. Although I think students nowadays write more than ever through the myriad social media tools available to them (the thought that goes into Instagram captions and Facebook posts is incredible!), that first step of putting pen or pencil to paper (or text key to screen) involves a little bit of self-faith that can be hard to muster! Luckily, there are brainstorming tools such as the RAFT to help students organize their thoughts just enough to begin responding to a prompt.

RAFT is a modest graphic organizer (the blank template is presented in Figure 2.1; a full-size template is provided at the end of the chapter) that does big things! After students receive a prompt, they can break it down to help define their role as a writer (R), the audience who will receive the writing (A), the format that the writing should take (F), and the topic that should be addressed (T) (Dean, 2006; Santa, Havens, & Valdes, 2004; Wilfong, 2014).

Figure 2.1 Blank RAFT

Role	Audience	Format	Topic

Figure 2.2 Completed RAFT

Role	Audience	Format	Topic
Grandpa, talking about the war	Family assembled around the table at Thanksgiving	Dialogue	Who is thankful for me? Story that shows this

This graphic organizer goes way beyond the webbing that students naturally turn to as a prewriting tool. It helps students frame their writing in a meaningful way that makes beginning writing "float" (get it?) to the page with ease. Figure 2.2 shows a completed RAFT graphic organizer in response to the first infinite prompt of Table 2.2, "Who is thankful for you? Tell a story that illustrates why this person feels this way."

What is so neat about the RAFT is the imagination that it provokes. Figure 2.2 is an actual completed RAFT to the "thankful" prompt by a preservice teacher I had in class. The topic of the RAFT had been provided by the prompt, and the student dutifully filled that in. To flesh out the writing, however, he pictured himself as an older gentleman telling a story about saving a comrade during combat (this student had recently completed a tour of duty in Afghanistan) to family gathered around the table at Thanksgiving. All of a sudden, we went from a basic response prompt to a story with depth, place, and meaning. This student later completed this prompt as an extended narrative for his writing portfolio (it was fabulous, by the way).

Updated Strategy #3: Framing Infinite Prompts for Specific Types of Writing: Argument, Informative, and Narrative

Under the Common Core State Standards, we know that students have three types of writing to master: argument/opinion, informative, and narrative. Argument writing and informative writing are shared by all content areas, whereas narrative is firmly planted in language arts (but bonus points to those creative social studies teachers who have shown fabulous narratives their students have written from a historical point of view!). For students to begin to try out techniques for all three types of writing, great prompts are necessary to give them the time and wiggle room to practice writing appropriately in the genre. Following is a discussion about each type of writing and sample infinite prompts to accompany them.

Narrative writing prompts. Narrative writing prompts are the first that teachers reach for when designing instruction. And it makes sense; narrative writing allows students to draw on personal experience and ideas to write about something that is meaningful. Do an Internet search for "writing prompts," and 90% of them will be for narrative writing (and then run an infinite/finite check on the prompt to ensure that it will solicit the kind of writing you wish!). But beyond Internet searches, there are a few other places I look for great, infinite narrative prompts:

Quotes: I do most things in life with either a notepad or my tablet next to me so that I can write down great quotes that I think will inspire writing in my students. Sometimes it is just a sentence or two from a book or magazine article; often it is something that I heard on TV or the radio. I keep these "nuggets" for just the right time or the right student. Here are a few of my favorites:

♦ "It is a fair, even-handed, noble adjustment of things, that while there is infection in disease, there is nothing in the world so irresistibly contagious as laughter and good humor" (*A Christmas Carol*).

♦ "I realize how quickly lies compound. They cover like a coat of paint, one on top of the other until you cannot remember what color you started with" (*Storytellers*, Jodi Picoult).

♦ "A life does not need to be human to be great" (Documentary, *A Whale Called Luna*).

Pictures and Images: Some of my favorite narrative writing from students has been in response to pictures. One in particular stands out—I posted a picture of a pretty white house with a striking red door. The varied responses were startling—students wrote about everything from divorce, to home maintenance, to murder. Several were taken to completion for their writing portfolios! A word of caution when using pictures: it is teacher nature to post the picture and then talk about it for 10 minutes (or more!) before letting students write. While it may feel right, the discussion that takes place might substitute for the original thoughts a student had about the picture. Let students write, and then let students share to prevent smothering of creativity!

Music/poetry: As illustrated by the "Springsteen" example, a song can evoke so much from our students. I have also had success with poetry, which allows students to talk about meaning and analysis and emotion without the fear of being "right" that clouds so much poetry reading in classrooms!

Informative writing prompts. Informative writing prompts for both bell work and extended writing in all classrooms are more difficult to make infinite. We often feel that writing to inform is limited by right and wrong answers or facts and end up crafting prompts in the "Name two . . ." or "Give an example" spirit. Instead, we can use personal connections as a jumping-off point to lead to true informative writing—for example:

- ◆ Describe the town where you live to someone who has never visited it.
- ◆ Nominate a figure from history as the most influential, including their impact on today's society (social studies specific).
- ◆ What is the single greatest invention of mankind? Why do you think this (science specific)?

Argument/Opinion writing prompts. The passion and spirit that underlie opinion and argument writing lend themselves well to infinite writing prompts for both bell work writing and extended writing experiences. To continue thinking about prompts that go beyond questions for response, I like to pick controversial topics and present them in unique formats. For example, electronic device use (and overuse) is a much-debated topic. I could merely present a prompt like this one:

> *Do we as a society overuse electronic devices like cell phones in our everyday lives?*

I would probably get pretty good responses because most students have a side to take on this topic. However, to provoke responses that allow for even more depth, I might give them an article, like "Teens Are Spending More Time Consuming Media on Mobile Devices" from the *Washington Post*, or watch a video on YouTube with them, like Louis C.K.'s brilliant rant about why he won't let his daughters have cell phones. Both the article and the video get at the basic question, but using them allows students to explore other sides to the argument and provides a basis for research necessary for completed argument papers on the topic.

Common Core Connection

The aforementioned strategies fit well with several Common Core State Standards for English Language Arts and Literacy Standards for History/Social Studies, Science, and Technical Subjects (see Tables 2.3 and 2.4).

Table 2.3 CCSS ELA Addressed in This Chapter

Grade Level	4–5	6–8	9–12
Standards Addressed	Write opinion pieces on topics or texts, supporting a point of view with reasons and information. Write informative/ explanatory texts to examine a topic and convey ideas and information clearly. Write narratives to develop real or imagined experiences or events using effective technique, descriptive details, and clear event sequences. Write routinely over extended time frames (time for research, reflection, and revision) and shorter time frames (a single sitting or a day or two) for a range of discipline-specific tasks, purposes, and audiences.	Write arguments to support claims with clear reasons and relevant evidence. Write informative/ explanatory texts to examine a topic and convey ideas, concepts, and information through the selection, organization, and analysis of relevant content. Write narratives to develop real or imagined experiences or events using effective technique, relevant descriptive details, and well-structured event sequences. Produce clear and coherent writing in which the development, organization, and style are appropriate to task, purpose, and audience.	Write arguments to support claims in an analysis of substantive topics or texts, using valid reasoning and relevant and sufficient evidence. Write informative/ explanatory texts to examine and convey complex ideas, concepts, and information clearly and accurately through the effective selection, organization, and analysis of content. Write narratives to develop real or imagined experiences or events using effective technique, well-chosen details, and well-structured event sequences.

Grade Level	4–5	6–8	9–12
	Produce clear and coherent writing in which the development and organization are appropriate to task, purpose, and audience.	Write routinely over extended time frames (time for research, reflection, and revision) and shorter time frames (a single sitting or a day or two) for a range of discipline-specific tasks, purposes, and audiences.	Produce clear and coherent writing in which the development, organization, and style are appropriate to task, purpose, and audience. Write routinely over extended time frames (time for research, reflection, and revision) and shorter time frames (a single sitting or a day or two) for a range of tasks, purposes, and audiences.

Table 2.4 CCSS Literacy Standards for History, Science, and Other Technical Subjects Presented in This Chapter

Grade Level	6–12
Standards Addressed	Write arguments focused on *discipline-specific content.* Write informative/explanatory texts, including the narration of historical events, scientific procedures/ experiments, or technical processes. Produce clear and coherent writing in which the development, organization, and style are appropriate to task, purpose, and audience. Write routinely over extended time frames (time for reflection and revision) and shorter time frames (a single sitting or a day or two) for a range of discipline-specific tasks, purposes, and audiences.

Conclusion

Using both infinite and finite writing prompts in our classrooms allows us to explore the many facets of writing response while helping our students to overcome the blank page or screen that they face at the beginning of every writing assignment. It's time to take some action . . .

Action Steps

1. Write down one writing prompt you have used in the past with students:

   _____

   a. Is it infinite or finite? How do you know? What type of writing did you want to elicit?

   _____

   _____

   b. If it is not the type of writing you wanted to elicit, change your prompt to make it more finite or infinite. Write the new prompt here:

   _____

   _____

2. Brainstorm one of each text type writing prompt to use in your classroom. Specify whether it is infinite or finite, depending on your purpose:

   a. Narrative:

   _____

   _____

   Infinite or finite? _____

   b. Argument/Opinion:

   _____

   _____

   Infinite or finite? _____

   c. Informative:

   _____

   _____

   Infinite or finite? _____

Works Cited

Calkins, L. (2010). *Launch an intermediate writing workshop: Getting started with units of study for teaching writing, grades 3–5*. Portsmouth, NH: Heinemann.

Carroll, S., & Feng, J. (2010). Writing prompts: The effect on first graders' writing ability and attitude towards writing. Paper presented at the Annual Meeting of the Georgia Educational Research Association, Savannah, October 22–23.

Dean, D. (2006). *Strategic writing: The writing process and beyond in the secondary English classroom*. Urbana, IL: NCTE.

Furtak, E. M., & Ruiz-Primo, M. A. (2008). Making students' thinking explicit in writing and discussion: An analysis of formative assessment prompts. *Science Education, 92*, 799–824.

Olinghouse, N. G., Zheng, J., & Morlock, L. (2012). State writing assessments: Inclusion of motivational factors in writing tasks. *Reading & Writing Quarterly, 28*, 97–119.

Santa, C., Havens, L., & Valdes, B. (2004). *Project CRISS: Creating independence through student-owned strategies*. Dubuque, IA: Kendall Hunt.

Wilfong, L. G. (2014). *Nonfiction strategies that work: Do this—not that!* New York: Routledge.

Template 2.1   RAFT Graphic Organizer

Role	Audience	Format	Topic

Role	Audience	Format	Topic

Have Students Read, Critique, and Learn From Master Authors in the Genre They Are Writing In

The writing contest was a runaway success. We had over 250 entries in three grade bands, all perfectly illustrating the theme, "The Internal Fear," in unique and interesting ways. We narrowed the entries down to three finalists and the final vote revealed the winners. I had the enviable task of notifying the teacher of each winner—my phone calls were met with squeals and happiness (always a nice thing to give a teacher on a regular school day). After getting particulars about where to send the prize, I had to pry: What motivated each student to write something so unique and moving, so wonderful? The answer was always the same: "We do a lot of reading of really great authors."

Why Is This Item on the List So Important?

The best writers we know are also some of the most voracious readers we know. We unconsciously absorb a writer's craft as we read and we apply these principles as we write. A child can correctly set up dialogue in writing without instruction if they are a reader—they see how it is supposed to be set apart with quotation marks, commas, and dialogue tags from a favorite author (or authors!) and use this knowledge in their own writing. So imagine what could happen if students are knowingly reading with an author's eye—paying attention to word choice, voice, and more with guidance from a teacher. The possibilities are endless!

> **Do this—not that principle #3:** DO have students read, critique, and learn from master authors in the genre they are writing. DON'T have students write without exposing them to readings from the genre.

To Get Started

Studying author's craft was intentionally included in the Common Core State Standards as an evidence-based (or research-based) practice (Troia & Olinghouse, 2013). And they are not where you might expect them: If you turn to the writing standards, you will see the writing genres, research, and proofreading. But turn back to the Reading Standards for Literature and Reading Standards for Informational Text; across the board, standards 4–6 examine Craft and Structure (CCSS, 2010). These standards analyze big choices that authors make:

1. Word choice (RL4 & RI4)
2. Text structure (RL5 & RI5)
3. Point of view and purpose (RL6 & RI6)

Beyond what is laid out in the reading standards, readers can examine so much more—sentence structure, voice, and figurative language are just a few of the ways that a reader can view a text (Dean, 2013). I find that it is often these elements of an author's craft that draw me to an author. True confession: I went through a pretty heavy L. M. Montgomery (of *Anne of Green Gables* fame) phase for roughly six years. The amount of figurative language that I included in my writing at that time was a bit over the top; yet when I was questioned by my teachers, and I mentioned my love for Lucy Maude, they got it. I was trying out what I was reading in my own writing.

There are students who do this innately; the majority of our students need to have their eyes opened to author's craft. A wonderful world of writing mentors awaits them!

A mentor text is any text from which a student can learn a writing technique (Culham, 2014; Fletcher & Portalupi, 2007; Gallagher, 2011). In this context, a text is loosely defined because writers can find inspiration anywhere:

Table 3.1 A Selection of Academic Books Addressing Mentor Texts

1. *Mentor texts: Teaching writing through children's literature, K-6.* Linda Dorfman & Rose Capelli.
2. *Craft lessons: Teaching writing, K-8* (2nd ed.). Ralph Fletcher & JoAnn Portalupi.
3. *The writing thief: Using mentor texts to teach the craft of writing.* Ruth Culham.
4. *Write like this: Teaching real-world writing through modeling and mentor texts.* Kelly Gallagher.

song lyrics, poetry, magazine articles, novels . . . really anything can be a mentor text. As a teacher using mentor texts in the classroom to teach the craft of writing, the key is to narrow down the focus to the one or two elements in which a particular text excels. I can then present it to my students through that lens—see how this author achieved this? We can analyze it, figure out why it was so powerful, and then see if this is something we want to steal for our own writing (Culham, 2014).

To me, mentor texts show the possibilities that exist in writing. Students often complain that writing is like conjuring up something out of nothing; they state that they feel isolated and at a loss for ideas. Mentor texts make writing techniques within reach for all students!

This chapter is not a list of mentor texts to use while teaching writing. There are many books out there that contain excerpts to use while teaching writing, along with accompanying minilessons. Table 3.1 presents a list of my favorite mentor text books—ones that I have relied upon to help me as I gathered my own favorite mentor authors and developed my own minilessons. What this chapter *has* is suggestions on how to begin reading like an author to find your own excerpts and develop your own minilessons for use in your Writers' Workshop.

Instructional Practices to Update

Updated Strategy #1: Consider Texts for Both Comprehension Instruction and Author's Craft That Meet the Genre You Are Emphasizing in Each Unit

For the majority of teachers out there, your school district provides a curriculum map, complete with a pacing guide that shows what book to use when. If you lack a curriculum map, you still have your anchor texts designated—that is, we read *The Outsiders* during first quarter, *Bomb! The Race to Build—and Steal—the World's Most Dangerous Weapon* during second quarter, and so forth. Or maybe you are in a true Readers' Workshop where students do not have a common text other than your daily read aloud (lucky you). In any case, you do hopefully have a text that all students have access to, one that you use on a regular basis in reading instruction. Your first purpose in using this text is to teach reading. As you read it yourself for the first time, think about what standards it can be used to instruct, how it meets the needs of your students, and how it interests and engages them. But for your second read, I want you to view this text through a writing teacher's eyes: Is this text in the genre on which I plan to focus my writing instruction during this unit? If it isn't, you may want to rethink your choice of text; reading in the genre is one of the best ways for students to get geared up to write. Now, still with your writing teacher's eyes, I want you to look at the list of minilessons you prepared from chapter 1 for the genre of writing you plan on teaching. Pen in hand, mark passages that show a specific element—is the beginning of a chapter or the book incredibly powerful? Mark that as a possibility for teaching good introductions. Is the structure of the article you plan on using in class set up in such a way that it makes organizing an essay easy to understand? Write that down. Reading with a pen in hand to mark writing techniques soon becomes second nature; even in books that I don't plan on using as a whole-class text, I read with a view to finding more and more excerpts, passages, and examples to teach writing techniques. Katie Wood Ray (2012) says that once you begin reading with writing in mind, you are forever changed (but in a good way!).

The second part to reading with a pen in hand is starting to archive this collection of excerpts, passages, and examples. I have a running document on my computer where I include the title of the text, page number, excerpt, and standard. What started as one or two excerpts has grown to hundreds; almost every time I read something, I am reading with two minds—one mind is to simply enjoy a book (because I still do that, too!). The other is to add to my collection of mentor texts. I now have a searchable document. I simply type in the key word of the lesson I am planning to teach (like voice or word choice), and I get to see all of the passages I previously identified that fit with that element.

Yes, I could simply buy a text that has mentor texts and their lessons already prepared for me. I don't know about you, but my students are simply not "one-size-fits-all." I was reminded of this the other day when

I was teaching an argumentative writing lesson to a group of high school students. I was using one of my favorite mentor texts, *Divergent*. We were imagining the inner argument Beatrice was having with herself, trying to choose her faction. I thought things were going swimmingly when one of the girls raised her hand. "Dr. Wilfong, no offense, but don't you have any books where the characters aren't white? Where they look like me, and talk like me, and have problems like me? This book seems good and all, but I can't relate." Shondra was giving voice to the problem with any prepared curriculum materials—it wasn't made with her in mind. There was no personalization of this lesson to these students; I chose it because I liked *Divergent*. The next time I went to Shondra's class, I combed through my collection to find something that fit her and her classmates. The engagement increased tenfold.

Content area mentor texts. With the advent of the Common Core Literacy Standards for History, Science, and Other Technical Subjects, writing is now an objective for all teachers, not just language arts teachers. Content area teachers in grades 6–12 have their own writing standards: writing informative/expository texts and writing arguments (CCSS, 2010). Mentor texts work just as well in content area classrooms as they do in language arts classrooms (Pytash, Edmonson Tait, 2014; Pytash & Morgan, 2014). In addition to teaching content, mentor texts in the content area classroom help scaffold the type of academic writing expected in that domain (Pytash & Morgan, 2014). For example, historians may structure a text different than a political scientist. An economist will use different vocabulary than will a geographer. Yet all of these academics—historian, political scientist, economist, and geographer—will be studied in a social studies classroom. A content area mentor text can help a student learn to write from a particular point of view and for a particular audience, adding depth to a piece.

Content area mentor texts encourage teachers to reach outside the textbook. Very rarely (or ever!) do we want our students to write like a textbook author. Instead, sources such as journal and newspaper articles, primary source documents, and biographies are great places for content area teachers to begin searching for the kinds of mentor texts that will lead to true academic writing.

Updated Strategy #2: Encouraging Students to Read for Author's Craft

As you begin using mentor texts to teach writing techniques, it is common to find the texts for your students to read. However, the students' own reading is a wealth of possibilities for finding hundreds more mentor authors. A little direction is needed to get them started, but soon students can become detectives of author's craft, themselves.

As stated earlier, the first read of a text is generally for comprehension and enjoyment. But a second read of a text (close reading alert!) can be done for writing techniques. Students are often drawn to a particular author because of style and voice, but they don't always have the words to express these techniques. A teacher once shared with me a set of two questions that allows older students to think about author's craft: Why this? Why here? If a student is reading and comes across a metaphor, they can ask themselves these two questions and without knowing it, they are studying author's craft. If they can answer those two questions, they are learning about the writing process in an inferential way: Why do I think the author used this technique? And why did they use it here, on this page, at this point in the story? These moments can be analyzed, shared, and displayed to allow students to see the myriad techniques that authors use in all texts, not just the ones you choose for them.

To make this strategy accessible for younger and struggling students, Hartman and Mooney (2013) tell teachers to set up a chart to help students pay attention to author "moves." This chart (Table 3.2) is an excellent way to begin an author's craft conversation that is supported in such a way that students can't help but be successful (a full-size chart is included at the end of the chapter).

Table 3.2 Paying Attention to Author Techniques: Sample Using *The One and Only Ivan* by Katherine Applegate

What is powerful?	Why is it powerful?	How did the author do this?
When Ivan is telling Ruby about his childhood.	Ivan is forced to reflect on what life was like before living at the mall.	By using simple language and powerful imagery, Applegate helps the reader understand more about Ivan.

Source: Adapted from Hartman and Mooney (2013).

The steps of the lesson are as follows:

1. The teacher reads aloud a text to students (it is helpful if students have copies or can follow along on a document camera).

2. After reading, the teacher asks a student to identify a favorite section. The section is reread.

3. The teacher goes through the questions on the chart, working with students to identify the technique (column 3) that made the writing so powerful.

4. At least three techniques are identified.

5. Students leave the lesson to either revise a current text they are writing or begin a new text, borrowing at least one of the techniques they learned from the mentor text in their own piece.

Updated Strategy #3: Using an Author Study to Delve Deeply Into an Admired Author's Craft

Once the purview of elementary school teachers, an author's study is a fabulous way to take an in-depth look at one author's writing techniques for use in our own writing. The reason this teaching practice is so common in elementary classrooms is because picture books lend themselves so well to an author's study—several can be read in a short period of time, and children's literature authors often have a signature technique (like Kevin Henke's asides in his books) that can easily be identified by young learners. But this practice is just as powerful with older students. Spending time with multiple works of literature by the same author allows students to become familiar with what makes an author timeless, popular—or both!

Another reason for including an author study with older students is that it invites inclusion by multiple levels of readers. Most authors have published works long and short, hard and easy. Suzanne Collins is a great example of this—we are all familiar with *The Hunger Games*, now a common read in most middle schools. But before *The Hunger Games*, Collins wrote the *The Underlander Chronicles* series, meant for a slightly less-mature audience. Students could select a text that fits their engagement level, but when it came time for writing, all students could identify and try out Collins's writing techniques in their own writing. There are several authors appropriate for middle/high school author studies; Table 3.3 lists a few of my favorite authors for author studies, along with a few titles you could use to implement this in your own classroom.

Figure 3.1 shows the steps in an author's study cycle appropriate for middle and high school readers.

Figure 3.1 An Author's Study Cycle for Author's Craft Identification

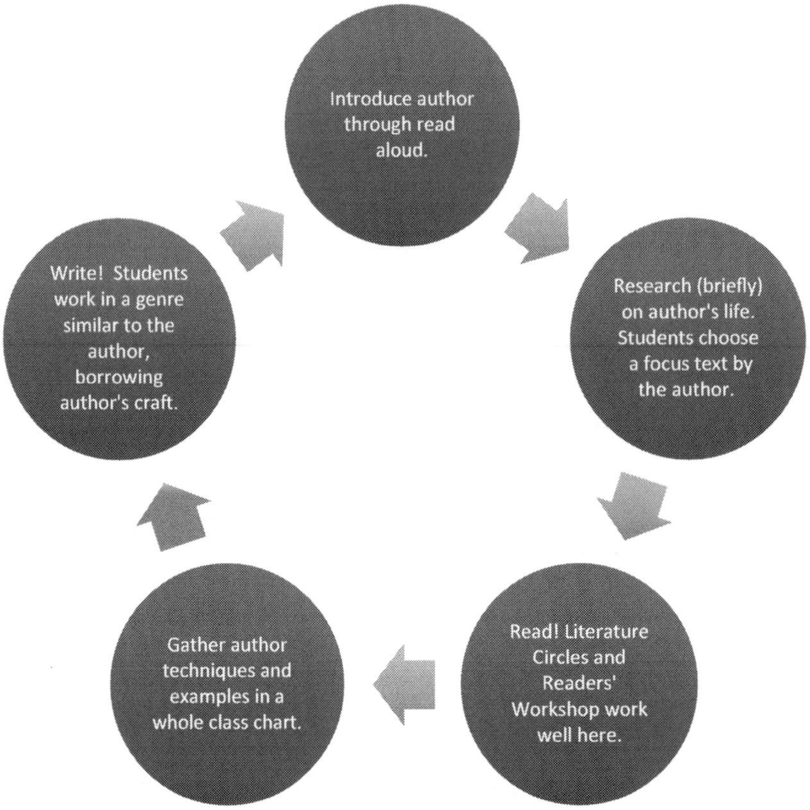

- Introduce author through read aloud.
- Research (briefly) on author's life. Students choose a focus text by the author.
- Read! Literature Circles and Readers' Workshop work well here.
- Gather author techniques and examples in a whole class chart.
- Write! Students work in a genre similar to the author, borrowing author's craft.

Table 3.3 Middle/High School–Appropriate Authors for Author's Study

Author	Suggested works
Mark Twain	*The Adventures of Tom Sawyer*; "The Celebrated Jumping Frog of Calaveras County" (short story); "A Dog's Tale" (short story)
Naomi Shihab Nye	*A Maze Me: Poems for Girls* (poetry); *Habibi* (novel); *There Is No Long Distance Now* (short stories)
Laurie Halse Anderson	*The Impossible Knife of Memory* (novel); *Speak* (novel); *Wintergirls* (novel)

Author	Suggested works
Steven Sheinkin	*Two Miserable Presidents: The Amazing, Terrible, and Totally True Story of the Civil War* (nonfiction); *Which Way to the Wild West?: Everything Your Schoolbooks Didn't Tell You about Westward Expansion* (nonfiction); *King George: What Was His Problem?: The Whole Hilarious Story of the American Revolution* (nonfiction)

Common Core Connection

Several standards (including all of the writing standards) fit well with the content of this chapter. However, it is the Craft and Structure Reading Standards that are fully impacted by the strategies discussed here (see Table 3.4).

Table 3.4 Craft and Structure Reading Standards

Grade Level	4	5	6
Standard Addressed	**Reading Standards for Literature** Determine the meaning of words and phrases as they are used in a text, including those that allude to significant characters found in mythology (e.g., Herculean). Explain major differences between poems, drama, and prose, and refer to the structural	**Reading Standards for Literature** Determine the meaning of words and phrases as they are used in a text, including figurative language such as metaphors and similes. Explain how a series of chapters, scenes, or stanzas fits together to provide the overall structure of a particular story, drama, or poem.	**Reading Standards for Literature** Determine the meaning of words and phrases as they are used in a text, including figurative and connotative meanings; analyze the impact of a specific word choice on meaning and tone. Analyze how a particular sentence, chapter, scene, or stanza fits into

(Continued)

Table 3.4 Continued

Grade Level	4	5	6
Standard Addressed	elements of poems (e.g., verse, rhythm, meter) and drama (e.g., casts of characters, settings, descriptions, dialogue, stage directions) when writing or speaking about a text. Compare and contrast the point of view from the difference between first- and third-person narrations. **Reading Standards for Informational Text** Determine the meaning of general academic and domain-specific words or phrases in a text relevant to a *grade 4 topic or subject area*. Describe the overall structure (e.g., chronology, comparison, cause/effect, problem/solution) of events, ideas, concepts, or	Describe how a narrator's or speaker's point of view influences how events are described. **Reading Standards for Informational Text** Determine the meaning of general academic and domain-specific words and phrases in a text relevant to a *grade 5 topic or subject area*. Compare and contrast the overall structure (e.g., chronology, comparison, cause/effect, problem/ solution) of events, ideas, concepts, or information in two or more texts. Analyze multiple accounts of the same event or topic, noting important similarities and differences in the point of view they represent.	the overall structure of a text and contributes to the development of the theme, setting, or plot. Explain how an author develops the point of view of the narrator or speaker in a text. **Reading Standards for Informational Text** Determine the meaning of words and phrases as they are used in a text, including figurative, connotative, and technical meanings. Analyze how a particular sentence, paragraph, chapter, or section fits into the overall structure of a text and contributes to the development of the ideas. Determine an author's point of view or purpose in a text and explain how it is conveyed in the text.

Grade Level	4	5	6
Standard Addressed	information in a textor part of a text. Compare and contrast a firsthand and secondhand account of the same event or topic; describe the differences in focus and the information provided.		

Grade Level	7	8	9–10

Standard Addressed	**Reading Standards for Literature** Determine the meaning of words and phrases as they are used in a text, including figurative and connotative meanings; analyze the impact of rhymes and other repetitions of sounds (e.g., alliteration) on a specific verse or stanza of a poem or section of a story or drama.
	
	    Analyze how a drama's or poem's form or structure (e.g., soliloquy, sonnet)
		Reading Standards for Literature Determine the meaning of words and phrases as they are used in a text, including figurative and connotative meanings; analyze the impact of specific word choices on meaning and tone, including analogies or allusions to other texts.
		
		    Compare and contrast the structure of two or more texts and analyze how the differing structure
			Reading Standards for Literature Determine the meaning of words and phrases as they are used in the text, including figurative and connotative meanings; analyze the cumulative impact of specific word choices on meaning and tone (e.g., how the language evokes a sense of time and place; how it sets a formal or informal tone).
			
			    Analyze how an author's choices concerning how

(*Continued*)

Table 3.4 Continued

Grade Level	7	8	9–10
Standard Addressed	contributes to its meaning. Analyze how an author develops and contrasts the points of view of different characters or narrators in a text. **Reading Standard for Informational Text** Determine the meaning of words and phrases as they are used in a text, including figurative, connotative, and technical meanings; analyze the impact of a specific word choice on meaning and tone. Analyze the structure an author uses to organize a text, including how the major sections contribute to the whole and to the development of the ideas. Determine an author's point of view or purpose	of each text contributes to its meaning and style. Analyze how differences in the points of view of the characters and the audience or reader (e.g., created through the use of dramatic irony) create such effects as suspense or humor. **Reading Standard for Informational Text** Determine the meaning of words and phrases as they are used in a text, including figurative, connotative, and technical meanings; analyze the impact of specific word choices on meaning and tone, including analogies or allusions to other texts. Analyze in detail the	to structure a text, order events within it (e.g., parallel plots), and manipulate time (e.g., pacing, flashbacks) create such effects as mystery, tension, or surprise. Analyze a particular point of view or cultural experience reflected in a work of literature from outside the United States, drawing on a wide reading of world literature. **Reading Standard for Informational Text** Determine the meaning of words and phrases as they are used in a text, including figurative, connotative, andtechnical meanings; analyze the cumulative impact of specific word choices on meaning and tone (e.g., how the language of

Grade Level	7	8	9–10
Standard Addressed	in a text and analyze how the author distinguishes his or her position from that of others.	structure of a specific paragraph in a text, including the role of particular sentences in developing and refining a key concept. Determine an author's point of view or purpose in a text and analyze how the author acknowledges and responds to conflicting evidence or viewpoints.	a court opinion differs from that of a newspaper). Analyze in detail how an author's ideas or claims are developed and refined by particular sentences, paragraphs, or larger portions of a text (e.g., a section or chapter). Determine an author's point of view or purpose in a text and analyze how an author uses rhetoric to advance that point of view or purpose.

Action Steps

Mentor texts are an amazing way to show your students the tools necessary to make writing come alive! It is time to take some action . . .

1. What is an anchor text that you commonly use with your students? Write the title here:

   _____

2. What writing genre does this best match up with (argument, informative/expository, or narrative)?

   _____

   _____

3. Look at the standards associated with this genre for your grade level. Skim your text; pick out three possible teaching points/standards in three separate passages. Write the page numbers and the teaching points/standards here:

   a. Teaching point/standard
      #1 _____
      Page number: _____

   b. Teaching point/standard
      #2 _____
      Page number: _____

   c. Teaching point/standard
      #3 _____
      Page number: _____

Works Cited

Culham, R. (2014). *The writing thief: Using mentor texts to teach the craft of writing.* Newark, DE: International Reading Association.

Dean, N. (2013). *Discovering voice: Voice lessons for middle and high school.* Gainesville, FL: Maupin House.

Dorfman, L., & Capelli, R. (2007) *Mentor texts: Teaching writing through children's literature, K-6.* Portland, ME: Stenhouse.

Fletcher, R., & Portalupi, J. (2007). *Craft lessons, second edition: Teaching writing, K-8.* Portland, ME: Stenhouse.

Gallagher, K. (2011). *Write like this: Teaching real-world writing through modeling and mentor texts*. Portland, ME: Stenhouse.

Hartman, A., & Mooney, J. (2013). *Lessons from the masters: Improving narrative writing*. Portsmouth, NH: Heinemann.

National Governors Association Center for Best Practices & Council of Chief State School Officers. (2010). *Common Core State Standards for English language arts and literacy in history/social studies, science, and technical subjects*. Washington, DC: Authors.

Pytash, K., Edmonson, E., & Tait, A. (2014). Using mentor texts for writing instruction in a high school economics class. *Social Studies Research and Practice, 9,* 95–106.

Pytash, K., & Morgan, D. (2014). Using mentor texts to teach writing in science and social studies. *Reading Teacher, 68,* 93–102.

Ray, K. (2012). Wondrous words. *Reading Teacher, 66,* 9–14.

Troia, G., & Olinghouse, N. (2013). The Common Core State Standards and evidence-based educational practices: The case of writing. *School Psychology Review, 42,* 343–357.

Template 3.1 Paying Attention to Author Techniques

What is powerful?	Why is it powerful?	How did the author do this?

Source: Adapted from Hartman and Mooney (2013).

Chapter 4

Create a Writing Community in Your Classroom

I approached creating writing groups with my preservice teachers with trepidation; how would they take to posting their writing online? Would they like commenting on each other's work? Would it turn into a popularity contest? Yet, I knew I wanted to give attention to their writing beyond my feedback. Four weeks later, our online community was thriving. Students were waiting with bated breath to read the next installment of a serial being written by a quiet student. Students were enjoying the encouragement from the peers and posting far more than I required. When I asked them why this was working out so well, Alicia put it best: "Dr. Wilfong, we do this kind of stuff all the time with Facebook and Instagram. It actually makes class feel more like our social lives. That's why we love it."

Why Is This Item on the List So Important?

Alicia's explanation is perfect: Our students are public writers already with the social media they use constantly. I once saw a student agonize over a 140-character tweet in a way that I am certain she did not agonize over a paper for class for me. The very act of writing for the majority of our students is already very social: they tweet, post, and caption their hearts out with an audience in mind. Writing a paper just for a teacher narrows their world down to a size that feels uncomfortable, with uncomfortable expectations. This is why creating a writing community in classrooms is paramount to writing success for so many of our students today—by opening up writing to a greater audience, you are mimicking the writing that students are already doing all the time.

If you just read that paragraph and felt a "Kids these days . . ." parable coming to your lips in the vein of, "In my day, we wrote with a number two pencil and lined paper and that was it! Whatever the teacher told us to do, we wrote it and we never expected any more feedback than her red pen," then look at it this way: There is only one of you. There are many of them. By developing a writing community, you are allowing students to find writing mentors in their peers who will offer advice and suggestions beyond what you can do in a normal school day. Students will begin to learn independence from the teacher—always a good thing! So embrace the 21st century as we turn to "Do this—not that" principle #4.

> **Do this—not that principle #4:** DO create a writing community in your classroom. DON'T have writing be an isolated, individual activity in your classroom.

To Get Started

There are sound, evidenced-based values behind writing communities, starting with everyone's favorite education researcher, Lev Vygotsky. The entire premise of workshop teaching is based on the Zone of Proximal Development: Students learn how to become writers based on what they need at that moment both conceptually and strategically (Bomer & Laman, 2004; Kesler, 2012). By giving students a writing community to participate in, we are placing them in "the zone" (Vygotsky, 1978). In fact, the very nature of group or partner work is based on scaffolding: allowing students to try out something new in a supported way until they are comfortable trying it out on their own (Wood & Middleton, 1975).

I find that many teachers are apprehensive about partner and group work, as well as online interaction (all used in this chapter) because they fear the lack of structure during these teaching times will lead to chaos. Here are a few ideas that always guide partner and group work in the successful writing classroom:

1. *Partnerships and group work are structured.* It is the rare seventh grader who will use group work time productively. Clear directions

must be given, a time limit must be set (and followed!), and accountability must be followed through on, with consequences for noncompliance.

2. *Norms of partner and group work are clearly explained.* It takes time to finesse good partnerships and group work. Many teachers like to use a "Looks like/sounds like" chart to show students how they are to act in these situations.

3. *Modeling and speaking frames are encouraged!* I find that many students simply do not have the language yet to participate in scholarly conversations, like those that can take place about writing. I encourage modeling the kinds of talk you wish to hear, using student examples of excellent student talk, and utilizing speaking frames to scaffold academic conversations (e.g., "I really like the way you use _____ (writing technique) in your writing. One way you could improve your writing is by _____.").

Instructional Practices to Update

Updated Strategy #1: Using Writing Partners Effectively to Create Community in the Classroom

Purposeful think-pair-share during everyday writing. For many of our students, writing in 7 minutes and 42 seconds is downright scary because of the push to start writing right away. Mentally scan your classroom right now: If you put a writing prompt up, how many of your students look like they have itchy fingers, they are so excited to write? How many are a bit more methodical, thinking through ideas before putting pen to paper? And how many are left staring at the ceiling or at their neighbor's paper, desperate for a good idea? This strategy is for those students in the last category.

Oral rehearsal has many benefits for the struggling student. Talking through a writing prompt allows a writing idea to take the fastest pathway from brain to mouth—students don't have to think of forming the perfect sentence or getting their hand set up in the right way. They can simply try out their idea and see a reaction from someone else.

I have seen teachers balk at this because they are afraid that the struggling students will simply borrow an idea from their partner rather than be forced to come up with their own. That is where the written think-pair-share comes in. Unlike a traditional think-pair-share, where students verbally share ideas with a partner without any writing (Vacca, Vacca, & Mraz, 2011), a written think-pair-share allows students to jot down a few ideas to bring to the meeting, holding both students equally accountable for a contribution (Wilfong, 2012). Using this strategy during everyday writing allows a struggling student time to develop their ideas, get meaningful feedback, and then head into Everyday Writing with a plan. Table 4.1 has a sample Think-Pair-WRITE template (a full-size template is located at the end of the chapter).

An aside with the Think-Pair-WRITE—put the prompt in the template BEFORE you hand it out to students for the activity. I find that students can spend 5 minutes just copying the prompt, leaving them very little time to plan their writing! Remove as many obstacles as possible so that they can get to the writing sooner.

An electronic writing partner. For some of our students, writing is more than just getting ideas; the physical act of writing can be a deterrent from writing. Assistive technology, like talk to text, can help remove the specter of physical writing for these students so that they can get ideas down and not worry about the mechanics (Caverly, 2008; Zascavage & Winterman, 2009). While assistive technologies are normally referenced for students with disabilities, I find that many students benefit from the use of talk to text technologies when brainstorming or drafting. A basic talk to text software allows a student to talk their ideas into a microphone (picture Madonna during the 1990s, singing with that black microphone on the side of her face). The computer translates the talk into text and produces a piece of writing that can be used for revising and editing. Generally, students have to end sentences with punctuation verbally for the program to pick it up; other than that minor detail, these programs are very accurate. I personally like the Dragon Dictation app, free to download to my phone; I can place my phone on a student desk and have them talk directly into it, and then I can email their text to a

Table 4.1 Everyday Writing Think-Pair-WRITE! Sample Completed Template

Writing Prompt	What I think I will write about	Additions to my idea after talking to my partner
Who is thankful for you?	My dog, because I feed and bathe her	Other ways I take care of her that she is grateful for: daily walks, couch snuggles, and treats!

computer for printing. No fancy Madonna microphone required! However, no software or program is perfect for every student; explore the options that abound and find one that is right for your school (Caverly, 2008).

I think of this kind of assistive technology as a digital writing partner. Students can get right to the business of writing by recording their thoughts and be immediately rewarded with something they have "written."

Writing Partners During Guided Writing

A long-sustaining writing partnership can be an asset during guided writing. And before you say, "My kids can't handle that!" witness suggestions from a first-grade writing unit that writing partnerships be established in first-grade classrooms in order for students to support each other (Calkins & Bleichman, 2003). A writing partner can be a motivator, sounding board, or a constructive critique—but a little instruction is required (Hsu, 2009).

The first step in creating this support system is establishing writing partners. I have seen teachers establish unit-long partnerships and weekly partnerships, or simply use "elbow buddies" (someone who is close enough to touch elbows with) for spur-of-the-moment conversations. In an established partnership, preliminaries are eliminated ("so, my paper is about"); conversations can be sustained over an entire piece, and changes can be shared, discussed, and celebrated as writing evolves. Matching kids up is tricky—do you let students choose? Assign partners based on writing competency? Assign a more proficient student with a struggling student? There are advantages and disadvantages to all three:

1. Allowing students to choose a writing partner ensures security in sharing information. During narrative writing, especially, students often share deeply meaningful personal experiences that they may be reluctant to share with someone outside of their inner circle. The disadvantage, of course, is that there will be students left out who end up being paired up, regardless of preference.

2. Assigning partners based on writing proficiency allows two higher-level writers to push each other to greater heights. It is a joy watching these students challenge each other to add more detail, more evidence, better word choices! The disadvantage can be two struggling writers paired up—more support will be needed for these pairs to help each other as writers beyond the basics.

3. Heterogeneous grouping (pairing a high student with a low student) can have benefits for both—a struggling student gets to have a great

model for writing and the more advanced student is able to reteach content, therefore strengthening their own knowledge. Another way to think of this kind of grouping is through strengths—one student may have great structure and organization but lacks style, while another may be bursting with style but lacks structure (Hsu, 2009). These two students are the prefect pairing! You just have to know your students well.

My recommendation? As you may have guessed, during the narrative writing unit, I allow students to choose their partners. During argumentative writing, I match students up based on ability. And during informative writing, I prefer to use heterogeneous grouping since my instruction may be more directed.

Fishbowling to scaffold academic conversations about writing. Once writing partnerships are established, there are so many ways to put them to use! Rather than trying to facilitate whole-class conversations on a particular element of writing, partnerships can be called upon to reflect upon instruction to strengthen writing. Here is an example of how that might work:

You teach a minilesson on sensory details. Your minilesson ends with students examining their drafts and thinking about how to apply sensory details to their writing. This is higher-level stuff! Usually, a student has already declared, "I'm done!" just by finishing a draft; you are asking them to revise something that they may feel is finished! Rather than just drifting into independent writing, use your writing partners. Giving a direction such as "Discuss with your writing partner at least two specific places in your writing where you can use sensory details. Highlight these in your writing so you know what you will do when writing time begins." Students can then use each other to make a plan.

I am often under the assumption that students are ready to have these kinds of conversations because my directions are clear enough. And many of my students are; they immediately turn toward each other and get to work. However, some of our students need explicit instruction on how to have these conversations, and that is where the Fishbowl strategy comes in (Young, 2007). Give a writing partnership directive like the one in the preceding paragraph. Circle around your class, listening for an excellent example of this conversation taking place. Stop the partnership conversations and invite students to listen in, taking note of how the conversation flows (Speaking and Listening standards alert!). These models will give students an idea of how an academic conversation, centered on writing, flows.

Table 4.2 lists other key moments to invoke partnership work to strengthen your Writers' Workshop.

Table 4.2 Key Moments for Writing Partners

Prior to Everyday Writing, to plan
After Everyday Writing, to share
During Guided Practice of a minilesson, to try out a new strategy
Prior to Independent Writing time, to plan
During Independent Writing time, to bounce off an idea
After Independent Writing time, for feedback

Updated Strategy #2: Using Writing Groups to Underscore That Writing Is Meant to Be Shared

I think one of the most nerve-wracking moments of my professional career was participating in a writing group as part of my experience as a participant in the National Writing Project. I brought my journal, with all of its collected writing, to our little room and sat down, worried about how my musings would be perceived. What started as nervousness evolved to my favorite time during the Summer Institute—I got honest feedback on the pieces I was writing, was delighted by the work of my fellow participants, and was encouraged to pursue ideas that I thought weren't enough (in fact, one of those ideas turned into my first book on vocabulary!).

Writing is meant to be shared! In the real world, people share writing with others and not with a teacher. When we assign writing and then just collect it, grade it, and return it, a student's voice is stifled. When we encourage feedback via face-to-face and electronic sharing, we are showing students their potential impact through their writing!

Creating face-to-face sharing opportunities during a writing unit. Just as sustained writing partnerships can motivate students during guided writing, a writing group can make writing even more impactful. Time is the biggest factor in trying to fit something like this in; however, I find that students benefit from regular writing group meetings. Fitting them in randomly does not show that you think these are a meaningful part of your writing classroom. In chapter 1, in the unit planners, you will see time on Fridays built in for the writing group. You may not want to do this weekly, but I would suggest that at the very least, bimonthly writing group meetings will allow students to feel like they are part of something bigger than writing for a grade.

Just as with writing partners, group makeup is important. The good thing here is that proficiency is not the key—writing groups are not the places to plan the minutia of a writing piece. When creating writing groups, I would instead look at personalities—can students feel comfortable sharing their writing with those in the group? And self-selection is not the way to go here:

students who are *too* close as friends will ignore the writing and talk about anything else under the sun.

A few norms are necessary to make writing groups work:

1. *A moderator/facilitator is key.* Just as you need a Discussion Director in Literature Circles, so you need someone in charge during writing group. This person makes sure that everyone shares and that everyone gives the kind of feedback the writer is seeking (more about that later). Once I establish my writing groups, I can then rotate the moderator role, complete with written participation guidelines, among the group during each meeting. Table 4.3 presents these guidelines to give to the moderator during writing group.

2. *Read your work—don't summarize your work.* One of the biggest slips a kid can make during writing group is to summarize their writing for the group instead of reading what they actually wrote. I see this all the time—I will call on a student after an Everyday Writing prompt to share what they wrote and they will respond with, "I wrote about . . ." I had to train my students to read what they wrote.

3. *No derogatory statements about your own work*! EVERYONE does this—before someone reads something they wrote, they say, "Well, this isn't very good," or, "You won't like it," or, "I wasn't sure where I was going with this," and then read with an apologetic air. I tell students they are not allowed to preface their work with anything other than the type of feedback they are seeking.

4. *Bless or press.* One of the greatest parts of our writing group in the National Writing Project was the use of these two words. Many people do not want criticism, even constructive criticism, of a piece

Table 4.3 Tips for Writing Group Moderators

As the moderator of writing group today, please keep these guidelines in mind:

1. Everyone should share something they are working on (within the time allotted).

2. Each writer should state prior to reading their piece whether they would like their piece "blessed" (praised) or "pressed" (given constructive feedback).

3. Everyone must contribute meaningful feedback to each writer.

4. Writers are not allowed to put down their writing!

from a peer. Or maybe they are just looking for encouragement to keep going. These students should ask that the rest of the group "bless" their piece; give it positive comments. Some students are ready for their writing to be challenged, strengthened, and added to. In this case, students would ask that the writing group "press" their piece.

5. *Specific feedback is required.* It is so easy to say, "I like that." It is so much harder to say, "I like that because . . ." Training students to give specific feedback forces them to listen closely. Generic feedback (even for students who simply want a piece "blessed") does nothing for the writer!

Creating electronic sharing opportunities. If fitting in bimonthly writing groups is not possible in your already crammed schedule, setting up an electronic sharing site may be a great option. Creating a space for students to post in-progress writing and receive feedback feels like the kind of writing they do in their social media–driven lives (Lacina & Griffith, 2012).

Finding the right site is the first step to host your classroom site; I used pbworks.com to set up a private, invitation-only site for my classroom. The very easy interface allowed me to create a page for each student and already came complete with space for students to comment on each other's writing. Figure 4.1 is a snapshot of our site homepage with the links to each student's space.

Figure 4.1   Sample Student Writing Share Site

Welcome to the Cohort 12 Writing Exchange!
We will use this site to post and respond to each other's writing.
Click on the link with your name to get started!

Jessica Allen	Sabrina Detchon	Jennifer Maley
	James Reed	Monic Scheible
Summer Carpenter	Blair Emler	Lacey McIntire
	Dr. Wilfong	
Nathan Cozart	Ashley Fazenbaker	Amanda Nicholas
	Marvita Starks	Michelle Peterson
Joseph Dale	Alicia Garner	Lauren Miller
	Kyle Stead	Alicia Harding
Stephanie Deisner	Sarah Hamilton	Sarah Pendleton
	Kelli Stephens	Matthew Denham
		Brenda Warner

My requirements with this site were simple; students had to submit one piece of writing in progress for each genre we were working on. They were then required to comment on three other students' writing per genre. We had a discussion about feedback, using Lacina and Griffith's explanation of "penny" and "dollar" comments on blog posts (2012). They say that a penny comment lacks substance, while a dollar comment will compliment something specific, make a connection to the writing, or ask questions to help the writer along (Lacina & Griffith, 2012). Yes, there were students who waited until the last minute to comment on each other's posts and post their own work, but as stated in the opening of this chapter, this thing had its own life force. Students urged each other on, got to know each other in ways that would never happen in our regular classroom, and felt proud of work they were producing.

And in case you didn't notice—my name is in the middle of our launch page. I submitted pieces I was working on right alongside my students, allowing them to comment on my work.

PBworks worked well for me, but there are myriad sites out there that will serve the same functions. As you are looking for a site to host your online writing community, keep these factors in mind:

- Can you keep track of who posts what? One of the biggest concerns I hear is about negative, anonymous comments. Sites that you can set up privately for your classroom almost always have this function, preventing cyberbullying and transparency in commenting.

- Easy uploading is important! I didn't want to have to worry about students struggling to get a piece of writing online. Most sites will accept multiple forms of electronic documents (e.g., Microsoft Word, PDF, GoogleDocs) for uploading, but many make you download the piece to your local computer for reading. Check your options.

- Is commenting automatic on each page? Or do you have to insert a comment scroll?

As you can see from Table 4.1, our site wasn't fancy, but it worked! Other than the necessities just listed, the rest of the bells and whistles are up to you!

Common Core Connection

The strategies described in this chapter fit well with a variety of Common Core State Standards (see Table 4.4).

Table 4.4 Common Core State Standards

Grade Level	4	5	6
Standard Addressed	**Writing** With guidance and support from peers and adults, develop and strengthen writing as needed by planning, revising, and editing. With some guidance and support from adults, use technology, including the Internet, to produce and publish writing as well as to interact and collaborate with others. **Speaking and Listening Standards** Engage effectively in a range of collaborative discussions (one-on-one, in groups, and teacher-led) with diverse partners on *grade 4 topics and texts,*	**Writing** With guidance and support from peers and adults, develop and strengthen writing as needed by planning, revising, editing, rewriting, or trying a new approach. With some guidance and support from adults, use technology, including the Internet, to produce and publish writing as well as to interact and collaborate with others. **Speaking and Listening Standards** Engage effectively in a range of collaborative discussions (one-on-one, in groups, and teacher-led) with diverse partners	**Writing** With some guidance and support from peers and adults, develop and strengthen writing as needed by planning, revising, editing, rewriting, or trying a new approach. Use technology, including the Internet, to produce and publish writing as well as to interact and collaborate with others. **Speaking and Listening Standards** Engage effectively in a range of collaborative discussions (one-on-one, in groups, and teacher-led) with diverse partners on *grade 6 topics, texts, and issues,*

(*Continued*)

Table 4.4   Continued

Grade Level	4	5	6
	building on others' ideas and expressing their own clearly. Follow agreed-upon rules for discussions and carry out assigned roles.	on *grade 5 topics and texts*, building on others' ideas and expressing their own clearly. Follow agreed-upon rules for discussions and carry out assigned roles.	building on others' ideas and expressing their own clearly. Follow rules for collegial discussions, set specific goals and deadlines, and define individual roles as needed.
Grade Level	**7**	**8**	**9–10**
	Writing With some guidance and support from peers and adults, develop and strengthen writing as needed by planning, revising, editing, rewriting, or trying a new approach, focusing on how well purpose and audience have been addressed. Use technology, including the Internet, to produce and publish writing	**Writing** With some guidance and support from peers and adults, develop and strengthen writing as needed by planning, revising, editing, rewriting, or trying a new approach, focusing on how well purpose and audience have been addressed. Use technology, including the Internet, to produce and publish writing	**Writing** Develop and strengthen writing as needed by planning, revising, editing, rewriting, or trying a new approach, focusing on addressing what is most significant for a specific purpose and audience. Use technology, including the Internet, to produce, publish, and update individual or shared writing products, taking advantage of technology's

Grade Level	7	8	9–10
	and link to and cite sources as well as to interact and collaborate with others, including linking to and citing sources. **Speaking and Listening Standards** Engage effectively in a range of collaborative discussions (one-on-one, in groups, and teacher-led) with diverse partners on *grade 7 topics, texts, and issues,* building on others' ideas and expressing their own clearly. Follow rules for collegial discussions, track progress towards specific goals and deadlines, and define individual roles as needed.	and present the relationships between information and ideas efficiently as well as to interact and collaborate with others. **Speaking and Listening Standards** Engage effectively in a range of collaborative discussions (one-on-one, in groups, and teacher-led) with diverse partners on *grade 8 topics, texts, and issues,* building on others' ideas and expressing their own clearly. Follow rules for collegial discussions and decision-making, track progress towards specific goals and deadlines, and define individual roles as needed.	capacity to link to other information and to display information flexibly and dynamically. **Speaking and Listening Standards** Initiate and participate effectively in a range of collaborative discussions (one-on-one, in groups, and teacher-led) with diverse partners on *grades 9–10 topics, texts, and issues,* building on others' ideas and expressing their own clearly and persuasively. Work with peers to set rules for collegial discussions and decision-making (e.g., informal consensus, taking votes on key issues, presentation of alternate views), clear goals and deadlines, and individual roles as needed.

Action Steps

Building a writing community is an important step toward making writing an integral part of your classroom! It is time to take some action . . .

1. Which type of community-building strategy would work best for your classroom: writing partners, face-to-face writing groups, or an online sharing site (or a combination)?

   _____

   _____

2. If you selected writing partners:
   a. How will you set up your partnerships?

      _____

      _____

   b. From Table 4.2, list at least two ways you will use these partnerships during your guided writing time:

      _____

      _____

3. If you selected face-to-face writing groups:
   a. How will you set up your groups?

      _____

      _____

   b. How often can you have them meet?

      _____

      _____

4. If you selected an online sharing site:
   a. How often will students be required to post writing?

      _____

      _____

   b. How often will students be required to comment on other students' writing?

      _____

      _____

   c. Will you award points for participation? How many? How often?

      _____

      _____

Works Cited

Bomer, R., & Laman, T. (2004). Positioning in a primary writing workshop: Joint action in the discursive production of writing subjects. *Research in the Teaching of English, 38*, 420–466.

Calkins, L., & Bleichman, P. (2003). The craft of revision. In L. Calkins (Ed.), *The units of study for primary writing* (pp. 91–98). Portsmouth, NH: Heinemann.

Caverly, D. (2008). Tech talk: Assistive technology for writing. *Journal of Developmental Education, 31*, 36–37.

Hsu, C. (2009). Writing partnerships. *Reading Teacher, 63*, 153–158.

Kesler, T. (2012). Writing with voice. *Reading Teacher, 66*, 25–29.

Lacina, J., & Griffith, R. (2012). Blogging as a means for crafting writing. *Reading Teacher, 66*, 316–320.

Vacca, R., Vacca J., & Mraz, M. (2011). *Content area reading: Literacy and learning across the curriculum.* New York: Pearson.

Wilfong, L. (2012). *Vocabulary strategies that work: Do this—not that!* New York: Routledge.

Wood, D., & Middleton, D. (1975). A study of assisted problem-solving. *British Journal of Psychology, 66*, 181–191.

Young, J. (2007). Small group scored discussions: Beyond the fishbowl, or everybody reads, everybody talks, everybody learns. *History Teacher, 40*, 177–181.

Zascavage, V., & Winterman, K. (2009). What middle school educators should know about assistive technology and universal design for learning. *Middle School Journal, 40*, 46–52.

Template 4.1 Everyday Writing Think-Pair-WRITE!

Writing prompt	What I think I will write about	Additions to my idea after talking to my partner

Chapter 5

Use Anchor Charts and Minilessons to Explicitly Teach Writing

Tania stared blankly at the checklist that her teacher had just passed out. She raised one hand, the list waving in the other. "Yes, Tania?" "Miss, I need to include all of these things in my paper?" Exasperated, the teacher sighed. "Yes, Tania. I explained that." Tania looked uncertainly at the list in front of her. "I don't know how to do all these things . . .," she trailed off. But the teacher had already moved on.

Why Is This Item on the List So Important?

When I debriefed with the teacher, she waved the checklist in front of me, not unlike Tania, in her frustration. "I took the rubric, put it in kid-friendly language and in a kid-friendly format. I am not sure what else to do." I replied gently, "Did you teach the items that are on the checklist?" She gave me a wide-eyed stare.

This small exchange perfectly exemplifies the idea of assigning versus teaching writing. For many of us, writing in middle school (and beyond) consisted of teachers assigning us a paper: The teacher stood at the front of the classroom and stated, "You have a five-page essay due on the imagery of *Romeo and Juliet* in two weeks." If you were a child of the rubric era, that assignment description was accompanied by a rubric to show expectations. You procrastinated on the assignment until the night before, stayed up into the wee hours and wrote, and, bleary-eyed, turned in something the next day (or was that just me?). You received back a paper covered in red ink, correcting your grammar. You might get a line at the bottom saying something vague like, "Good job! Good description of imagery." You let it fester at the bottom of your backpack and waited for the next assignment.

Teaching writing as a process, not an end product, is what so many teachers are missing. And at the heart of this process is using the teaching tools of anchor charts and minilessons to show students exactly *how* to write.

> Do this—not that principle #5: DO use anchor charts and mini-lessons to explicitly teach writing. DON'T only give rubrics or checklists to show what is required in a piece of writing.

To Get Started

Minilessons and anchor charts are all about the gradual release of responsibility model. Through the use of this model, teachers are prompted to plan how to transition from heavy support and teaching by gradually releasing responsibility so that students assume responsibility for their learning (Duke & Pearson, 2002; Grant et al., 2012). Rather than using an interrogational mode of learning (Me—Teacher. You—student. I teach, you learn. Then I test you to see if you learn what I teach), you are providing the scaffolding necessary for a student to try out increasingly difficult tasks in their writing (Benko, 2012). Gradual release of responsibility is often referred to as "I do, we do, you do" (Grant et al., 2012).

The original purpose of scaffolding was to help students become masters of something (strategy, technique, idea, content) so that they could apply it under a different context (Langer & Applebee, 1986). This fits so perfectly with teaching writing as process: We are showing students the craft that they need to become masterful, independent writers.

Instructional Practices to Update

Updated Strategy #1: Designing Effective, Focused Minilessons to Teach Elements of a Genre

I believe that one of the reasons that teachers get so overwhelmed at the idea of teaching writing is that they feel like they must do everything at once: I must teach voice, word choice, and conclusions in a single shot, while worrying about conventions and mechanics. Really great minilessons are truly focused on ONE technique of great writers (Calkins, 1994; Atwell, 1987).

Portrait of a minilesson. Let's break a minilesson down into its three basic parts:

1. *Model.* I start a minilesson by presenting a piece of writing that I am working on. This is vital to the writing process. If I take risks, sharing my writing with my students, then they will be more likely to take their own risks in their own writing (Kittle, 2008; Street, 2005). I display my piece for student viewing and read it aloud, inviting them into a writer's conversation. Then, I talk about the technique that we are studying for today. I might define it, I might make an anchor chart (strategy #2 in this chapter!), we might look at examples of authors doing this well (mentor texts!), or we might just get right to the lesson. Thinking aloud, I walk my students through how I might apply this technique to my own writing. Thinking aloud is vital—I am very explicitly showing students how I change my writing, and how to make it better using this strategy. I write in front of them, crossing out what I am changing (or deleting if I am using the computer) and writing in my changes, modeling exactly how revision takes place. My thinking aloud is modeling writer metacognition, telling them my thought process so they can try it out themselves (Frey & Fisher, 2009). Students are following along during this part of the lesson. You might have them take notes on the technique; I find that if I am engaging them through my thinking aloud, it is enough to have them just absorb what I am doing.

2. *Guided practice.* After I have modeled the technique, it is time for the "we do" of the gradual release of responsibility model (Grant et al., 2012). This provides a low-risk opportunity for students to try out this technique (Fisher & Frey, 2009). Often using my model

writing, I will ask students, working with an elbow buddy or table group, to apply the technique to another part of the text. Using a sample of teacher writing is powerful; what student doesn't love the chance to show up the teacher? I am happy to let them change my writing, because this is my opportunity to see if students are ready to try this out on their own. This group or partner work is timed; depending on the task, I give them anywhere from 3 to 10 minutes to apply the technique to the writing sample. We then go around the room, sharing our revisions. There is great formative assessment happening at this juncture—I am able to see which students are able to move onto to the next step, independent practice.

3. *Independent practice.* After guided practice, it is time to get the application part of writing started. I direct students to look at their own writing and make a plan on how they will apply this writing technique. "I won't" is not an answer! Depending on student proficiency, I may make a recommendation for application, based on my expectations from their pre-unit on-demand assessment. This allows me to differentiate the lesson outcome for each student. The depth of application may differ, too; for example, in argument writing, the amount of evidence required can vary by student ability. Plans are made (perhaps with a writing partner) and writing begins. If I identified students during guided practice who were not yet ready to try out this technique or idea on their own, I now have the time to pull a small group together and reteach the lesson without holding the rest of the students back.

Figure 5.1   Blank Minilesson Template

Unit/Genre: _____
Complete standard: _____   _____
Portion of the standard for emphasis in this lesson: _____   _____
Modeling:
Guided Practice:
Directions for Independent Practice:
Reteaching ideas:

Go back to chapter 1, where you looked at the standard of a particular genre of writing and broke it down into individual lessons to teach. This is where the basis for your lessons will come from. Also, look at the rubric you will use for your guided writing and on-demand assessment—if it is on the rubric, it needs to be a minilesson! This includes grammar and mechanics—each aspect of the writing conventions can be broken down into a minilesson and applied in the same manner to student writing.

In each of the writing genre chapters (chapter 8—Narratives, chapter 9—Informational/Expository, and chapter 10—Argument), I will provide a sample minilesson that could be applied across grade levels. Enjoy trying them out with your own students as you begin to develop your own! Figure 5.1 is a blank writing minilesson template. A full-sized template is included at the end of the chapter.

Updated Strategy #2: Using Anchor Charts as a Contract Between Teacher and Student About Writing Expectations in a Genre

If you are into Pinterest, look up "writing anchor charts"—thousands of "pins" abound! Once the purview of elementary school teachers everywhere, anchor charts have crept into the intermediate, middle, and high school classroom as a way to publicly document the writing expectations taught in each minilesson (Boushey & Mosey, 2014).

Anchor charts are pretty simple (contrary to some of the examples I saw on Pinterest). Figure 5.2 is a suggested anchor chart template to use when planning your minilessons (a full-size template is included at the end of the chapter). As stated earlier, anchor charts are usually invoked during the modeling phase of your lesson—after you name your teaching point, an anchor chart can be used to do the (very short) transmission of knowledge on the technique you are about to teach. You may not always use all pieces and parts when creating one with your students.

Figure 5.2 Blank Anchor Chart Template

Item
Definition:
Mentor text examples:
Student examples:

Figure 5.3 is a picture of an anchor chart created by a fourth-grade teacher teaching a lesson on capitalization.

There is nothing fancy about this (in fact, the teacher didn't want me to use her name in conjunction with this anchor chart!). But I liked it *because* of its simplicity: It names the teaching point and lists suggestions the students made for things that need capital letters in their writing.

I think of anchor charts as almost a contract between teacher and student. My minilessons produce an artifact that can hang on the walls, a solid

Figure 5.3   Sample Anchor Chart

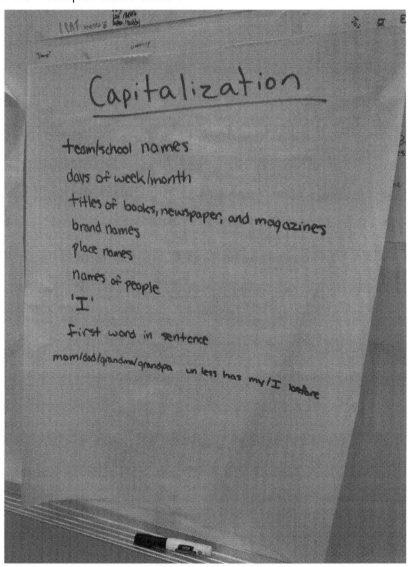

reminder of what I expect to be included in their writing. But more than that, they provide a student with a place to look for ideas and examples of how to change their writing.

To create great anchor charts, you only need chart or butcher paper and a marker. Do not fret about perfect handwriting or buying the expensive pads of chart paper with the sticky top—the chart that is produced is all that matters! With each minilesson, I suggest that you have a blank chart naming the teaching point ready to go; the rest can be provided by the students throughout your lesson. If you are a Smart Board kind of a person, you can absolutely create your charts via computer—the thing to keep in mind is how you will either print these out to distribute to students to keep in a notebook or folder (loose/lost paper alert!) or borrow a colleague's idea: She created charts on her computer with her students and then e-mailed them to a discount store that would enlarge and print them out for her to post in her classroom (she couldn't stand the sight of her writing covering the classroom). It made for a neat visual reminder of her lessons.

How long do anchor charts stay up? If they are truly specific to a single genre, then they stay up as long as the unit lasts. However, if the technique taught during a minilesson endures across genres, let it stay up as long as it is needed!

Figure 5.4 has a collage of some of the best anchor charts that I have seen in classrooms.

Figure 5.4 More Sample Anchor Charts

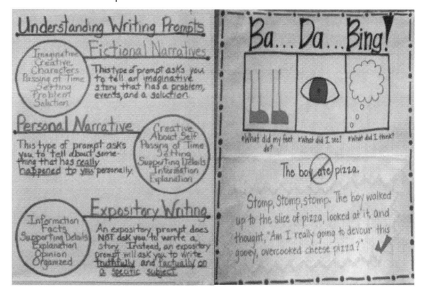

Common Core Connection

Minilessons and anchor charts are the explicit teaching that happen to make the writing process work in the classroom. They can cover any and all of the standards for writing (see Table 5.1).

Table 5.1 Writing Standards

Grade Level	4	5	6
Standard Addressed	**Writing** Write opinion pieces on topics or texts, supporting a point of view with reasons and information. Introduce a topic or text clearly, state an opinion, and create an organizational structure in which related ideas are grouped to support the writer's purpose. Provide reasons that are supported by facts and details. Link opinion and reasons using words and phrases (e.g., *for instance, in order to, in addition*). Provide a concluding statement or section related to the opinion presented.	**Writing** Write opinion pieces on topics or texts, supporting a point of view with reasons and information. Introduce a topic or text clearly, state an opinion, and create an organizational structure in which ideas are logically grouped to support the writer's purpose. Provide logically ordered reasons that are supported by facts and details. Link opinion and reasons using words, phrases, and clauses (e.g., *consequently, specifically*). Provide a concluding statement or	**Writing** Write arguments to support claims with clear reasons and relevant evidence. Introduce claim(s) and organize the reasons and evidence clearly. Support claim(s) with clear reasons and relevant evidence, using credible sources and demonstrating an understanding of the topic or text. Use words, phrases, and clauses to clarify the relationships among claim(s) and reasons. Establish and maintain a formal style. Provide a concluding statement or

Grade Level	4	5	6
	Write informative/ explanatory texts to examine a topic and convey ideas and information clearly. Introduce a topic clearly and group related information in paragraphs and sections; include formatting (e.g., headings), illustrations, and multimedia when useful to aiding comprehension. Develop the topic with facts, definitions, concrete details, quotations, or other information and examples related to the topic. Link ideas within categories of information using words and phrases (e.g., *another, for example, also, because*). Use precise language and domain-specific vocabulary to inform about or explain the topic.	section related to the opinion presented. Write informative/ explanatory texts to examine a topic and convey ideas and information clearly. Introduce a topic clearly, provide a general observation and focus, and group related information logically; include formatting (e.g., headings), illustrations, and multimedia when useful to aiding comprehension. Develop the topic with facts, definitions, concrete details, quotations, or other information and examples related to the topic. Link ideas within and across categories of information using words, phrases,	section that follows from the argument presented. Write informative/ explanatory texts to examine a topic and convey ideas, concepts, and information through the selection, organization, and analysis of relevant content. Introduce a topic; organize ideas, concepts, and information, using strategies such as definition, classification, comparison/ contrast, and cause/effect; include formatting (e.g., headings), graphics (e.g., charts, tables), and multimedia when useful to aiding comprehension. Develop the topic with relevant facts, definitions, concrete details, quotations, or other information and examples.

(*Continued*)

Table 5.1 Continued

Grade Level	4	5	6
	Provide a concluding statement or section related to the information or explanation presented. Write narratives to develop real or imagined experiences or events using effective technique, descriptive details, and clear event sequences. Orient the reader by establishing a situation and introducing a narrator and/or characters; organize an event sequence that unfolds naturally. Use dialogue and description to develop experiences and events or show the responses of characters to situations. Use a variety of transitional words and phrases to manage the sequence of events.	and clauses (e.g., *in contrast, especially*). Use precise language and domain-specific vocabulary to inform about or explain the topic. Provide a concluding statement or section related to the information or explanation presented. Write narratives to develop real or imagined experiences or events using effective technique, descriptive details, and clear event sequences. Orient the reader by establishing a situation and introducing a narrator and/or characters; organize an event sequence that unfolds naturally. Use narrative techniques, such as dialogue,	Use appropriate transitions to clarify the relationships among ideas and concepts. Use precise language and domain-specific vocabulary to inform about or explain the topic. Establish and maintain a formal style. Provide a concluding statement or section that follows from the information or explanation presented. Write narratives to develop real or imagined experiences or events using effective technique, relevant descriptive details, and well-structured event sequences. Engage and orient the reader by establishing a context and introducing a

Grade Level	4	5	6
	Use concrete words and phrases and sensory details to convey experiences and events precisely.
Provide a conclusion that follows from the narrated experiences or events.
Write routinely over extended time frames (time for research, reflection, and revision) and shorter time frames (a single sitting or a day or two) for a range of discipline-specific tasks, purposes, and audiences.	description, and pacing, to develop experiences and events or show the responses of characters to situations.
Use a variety of transitional words, phrases, and clauses to manage the sequence of events.
Use concrete words and phrases and sensory details to convey experiences and events precisely.
Provide a conclusion that follows from the narrated experiences or events.
Write routinely over extended time frames (time for research, reflection, and revision) and shorter time frames (a single sitting or a day or two) for a range of discipline-specific tasks, purposes, and audiences.	narrator and/or characters; organize an event sequence that unfolds naturally and logically.
Use narrative techniques, such as dialogue, pacing, and description, to develop experiences, events, and/or characters.
Use a variety of transition words, phrases, and clauses to convey sequence and signal shifts from one time frame or setting to another.
Use precise words and phrases, relevant descriptive details, and sensory language to convey experiences and events.
Provide a conclusion that follows from the narrated experiences or events.
Write routinely over extended time frames (time for

(Continued)

Table 5.1 Continued

Grade Level	4	5	6
			research, reflection, and revision) and shorter time frames (a single sitting or a day or two) for a range of discipline-specific tasks, purposes, and audiences.

Grade Level	7	8	9–10
	Writing Write arguments to support claims with clear reasons and relevant evidence.　Introduce claim(s), acknowledge alternate or opposing claims, and organize the reasons and evidence logically.　Support claim(s) with logical reasoning and relevant evidence, using accurate, credible sources and demonstrating an understanding of the topic or text.　Use words, phrases, and	**Writing** Write arguments to support claims with clear reasons and relevant evidence.　Introduce claim(s), acknowledge and distinguish the claim(s) from alternate or opposing claims, and organize the reasons and evidence logically.　Support claim(s) with logical reasoning and relevant evidence, using accurate, credible sources and demonstrating an understanding of the topic or text.	**Writing** Write arguments to support claims in an analysis of substantive topics or texts, using valid reasoning and relevant and sufficient evidence.　Introduce precise claim(s), distinguish the claim(s) from alternate or opposing claims, and create an organization that establishes clear relationships among claim(s), counterclaims, reasons, and evidence.　Develop claim(s) and counterclaims

Grade Level	7	8	9–10
	clauses to create cohesion and clarify the relationships among claim(s), reasons, and evidence. Establish and maintain a formal style. Provide a concluding statement or section that follows from and supports the argument presented. Write informative/ explanatory texts to examine a topic and convey ideas, concepts, and information through the selection, organization, and analysis of relevant content. Introduce a topic clearly, previewing what is to follow; organize ideas, concepts, and information, using strategies such as definition, classification, comparison/	Use words, phrases, and clauses to create cohesion and clarify the relationships among claim(s), counterclaims, reasons, and evidence. Establish and maintain a formal style. Provide a concluding statement or section that follows from and supports the argument presented. Write informative/ explanatory texts to examine a topic and convey ideas, concepts, and information through the selection, organization, and analysis of relevant content. Introduce a topic clearly, previewing what is to follow; organize ideas, concepts, and	fairly, supplying evidence for each while pointing out the strengths and limitations of both in a manner that anticipates the audience's knowledge level and concerns. Use words, phrases, and clauses to link the major sections of the text, create cohesion, and clarify the relationships between claim(s) and reasons, between reasons and evidence, and between claim(s) and counterclaims. Establish and maintain a formal style and objective tone while attending to the norms and conventions of the discipline in which they are writing. Provide a concluding statement or section that follows from and supports the argument presented.

(*Continued*)

Table 5.1 Continued

Grade Level	7	8	9–10
	contrast, and cause/ effect; include formatting (e.g., headings), graphics (e.g., charts, tables), and multimedia when useful to aiding comprehension. Develop the topic with relevant facts, definitions, concrete details, quotations, or other information and examples. Use appropriate transitions to create cohesion and clarify the relationships among ideas and concepts. Use precise language and domain-specific vocabulary to inform about or explain the topic. Establish and maintain a formal style. Provide a concluding statement or section that follows from and supports	information into broader categories; include formatting (e.g., headings), graphics (e.g., charts, tables), and multimedia when useful to aiding comprehension. Develop the topic with relevant, well-chosen facts, definitions, concrete details, quotations, or other information and examples. Use appropriate and varied transitions to create cohesion and clarify the relationships among ideas and concepts. Use precise language and domain-specific vocabulary to inform about or explain the topic. Establish and maintain a formal style. Provide a concluding	Write informative/ explanatory texts to examine and convey complex ideas, concepts, and information clearly and accurately through the effective selection, organization, and analysis of content. Introduce a topic; organize complex ideas, concepts, and information to make important connections and distinctions; include formatting (e.g., headings), graphics (e.g., figures, tables), and multimedia when useful to aiding comprehension. Develop the topic with well-chosen, relevant, and sufficient facts, extended definitions, concrete details, quotations, or

Grade Level	7	8	9–10

	the information or explanation presented.
	
	    Write narratives to develop real or imagined experiences or events using effective technique, relevant descriptive details, and well-structured event sequences.
	
	    Engage and orient the reader by establishing a context and point of view and introducing a narrator and/or characters; organize an event sequence that unfolds naturally and logically.
	
	    Use narrative techniques, such as dialogue, pacing, and description, to develop experiences, events, and/or characters.
	
	    Use a variety of transition words, phrases, and clauses to convey sequence and signal shifts from
		statement or section that follows from and supports the information or explanation presented.
		
		    Write narratives to develop real or imagined experiences or events using effective technique, relevant descriptive details, and well-structured event sequences.
		
		    Engage and orient the reader by establishing a context and point of view and introducing a narrator and/or characters; organize an event sequence that unfolds naturally and logically.
		
		    Use narrative techniques, such as dialogue, pacing, description, and reflection, to develop experiences,
			other information and examples appropriate to the audience's knowledge of the topic.
			
			    Use appropriate and varied transitions to link the major sections of the text, create cohesion, and clarify the relationships among complex ideas and concepts.
			
			    Use precise language and domain-specific vocabulary to manage the complexity of the topic.
			
			    Establish and maintain a formal style and objective tone while attending to the norms and conventions of the discipline in which they are writing.
			
			    Provide a concluding statement or section that follows from and supports the information

(*Continued*)

Table 5.1 Continued

Grade Level	7	8	9–10
	one time frame or setting to another. Use precise words and phrases, relevant descriptive details, and sensory language to capture the action and convey experiences and events. Provide a conclusion that follows from and reflects on the narrated experiences or events. Write routinely over extended time frames (time for research, reflection, and revision) and shorter time frames (a single sitting or a day or two) for a range of discipline-specific tasks, purposes, and audiences.	events, and/or characters. Use a variety of transition words, phrases, and clauses to convey sequence, signal shifts from one time frame or setting to another, and show the relationships among experiences and events. Use precise words and phrases, relevant descriptive details, and sensory language to capture the action and convey experiences and events. Provide a conclusion that follows from and reflects on the narrated experiences or events. Write routinely over extended time frames (time for research, reflection, and revision) and	or explanation presented (e.g., articulating implications or the significance of the topic). Write narratives to develop real or imagined experiences or events using effective technique, well-chosen details, and well-structured event sequences. Engage and orient the reader by setting out a problem, situation, or observation, establishing one or multiple point(s) of view, and introducing a narrator and/ or characters; create a smooth progression of experiences or events. Use narrative techniques, such as dialogue, pacing, description, reflection, and multiple plot lines, to develop

Grade Level	7	8	9–10
		shorter time frames (a single sitting or a day or two) for a range of discipline-specific tasks, purposes, and audiences.	experiences, events, and/or characters. Use a variety of techniques to sequence events so that they build on one another to create a coherent whole. Use precise words and phrases, telling details, and sensory language to convey a vivid picture of the experiences, events, setting, and/or characters. Provide a conclusion that follows from and reflects on what is experienced, observed, or resolved over the course of the narrative. Write routinely over extended time frames (time for research, reflection, and revision) and shorter time frames (a single sitting or a day or two) for a range of tasks, purposes, and audiences.

Action Steps

Anchor charts and minilessons are the key to good teaching during Guided Writing. It's time to take some action . . .

1. One of the bases of a good minilesson is writing in front of your students during the modeling phase and then letting students use your writing during guided practice to apply the technique being taught. What is your initial reaction to this idea?

   _____

   _____

2. Take a look at the prompts you created in chapter 2. Which prompt do you think will produce *your* best writing? Why?

   _____

   _____

3. Now, match that prompt up with a standard-based minilesson. What writing technique could be taught in conjunction with that prompt?

   _____

   _____

4. Finally, prepare for your anchor chart to go with this lesson:
   a. Define the technique in student-friendly terms:

   _____

   _____

   b. See if you can find two or three mentor text examples of this technique:

   Author, title, page number: _____

   Author, title, page number: _____

   Author, title, page number: _____

Works Cited

Atwell, N. (1987). *In the middle: Writing, reading, and learning with adolescents.* Portsmouth, NH: Heinemann.

Benko, S. (2012). Scaffolding: An ongoing process to support adolescent writing development. *Journal of Adolescent and Adult Literacy, 56,* 291–300.

Boushey, G., & Mousey, J. (2014). *The daily 5: Fostering literacy in the elementary grades.* New York: Stenhouse.

Calkins, L. (1994). *The art of teaching writing.* Portsmouth, NH: Heinemann.

Duke, N. K., & Pearson, P. D. (2002). Effective practices for developing reading comprehension. In A. E. Farstup & S. J. Samuels (Eds.), *What research has to say about reading instruction* (pp. 205–242). Newark, DE: International Reading Association.

Frey, N., & Fisher. D. (2009). The release of learning. *Principal Leadership, 9,* 18–22.

Grant, M., Lapp, D., Fisher, D., Johnson, K., & Frey, N. (2012). Purposeful instruction: Mixing up the "I," "we," and "you." *Journal of Adolescent and Adult Literacy, 56,* 45–55.

Kittle, P. (2008). *Write beside them: Risk, voice, and clarity in high school writing.* Portsmouth, NH: Heinemann.

Langer, J., & Applebee, A. N. (1986). Reading and writing instruction: Toward a theory of teaching and learning. *Review of Research in Education, 13,* 171–194.

Street, C. (2005). A reluctant writer's entry into a community of writers. *Journal of Adolescent & Adult Literacy, 48,* 636–641.

Template 5.1 Writing Minilesson Template

Unit/Genre: _____

Complete standard:

_____

_____

_____

_____

Portion of the standard for emphasis in this lesson:

_____

_____

Modeling:

Guided Practice:

Directions for Independent Practice:

Reteaching ideas:

Item
Definition:
Mentor text examples:
Student examples:

Chapter 6

Emphasize Content and Revision When Helping Students Develop as Writers, Teaching Editing in Context of the Student Writing

The teacher shoved a student paper under my nose. "Tell me what I am supposed to do with something like this!" she requested. I took the paper and looked over a confusion of red pen, crossed-out words, and scribbled comments. A big red "F" adorned the top. "Why did this student receive an F?" I asked. She pointed to all the red cross-outs on the paper. "The spelling! It's atrocious! She can't write at all." I read the story. It was a magnificent narrative—engaging introduction, developed plot, interesting characters. I looked up at the teacher, confused. "This is a really good story. What was used to grade this?" She responded, "We look at the important things: spelling, grammar, handwriting, and legibility."

Why Is This Item on the List So Important?

What makes good writing? This is something each teacher has to define for him- or herself. For the teacher in the anecdote, writing is good mechanics.

When she showed me the rubric, punctuation and capitalization were also emphasized. I did not ask the student who composed the piece what she thought made a good writer, but it is likely that she had absorbed the same ideas that her teacher was imposing (Zumbrunn & Krause, 2012).

If you follow the process laid out in this book, you know that I believe that content should be the emphasis of the writing process we share with students. We have to show our students that they have something to say and give them space and time to say it—Everyday Writing accomplishes this. Then, through Guided Writing, we show them how to take their first attempts and turn them into a polished piece of writing through revision and editing minilessons.

Teachers have this need, this yearning, to take a piece of writing from a student and fix it. It is like our fingers are itching to correct spelling, verb tense, and punctuation usage. And yet when you ask someone about their negative writing memories, they remember receiving a piece of writing back from a teacher covered in red pen, all their minute mistakes corrected, with vague feedback about the writing itself.

I would like you to let go of the practice of taking home stacks of rough drafts and "fixing them." Instead, I would like you to think about how you can empower students to take responsibility for their own writing through instructional practices like the ones introduced in this chapter.

> **Do this—not that principle #6:** DO emphasize content and revision when helping students develop as writers, teaching editing in context of the student writing. DON'T skip or limit revising strategies in favor of isolated editing drills while only emphasizing language while grading.

To Get Started

Writing instruction is an issue of control for so many teachers (Fisher, 2006). You want to dictate a topic, pick a graphic organizer, support students as they are writing paragraphs (with the number of paragraphs and sentences determined for students to write to earn full points), and then take papers home to correct before returning them to students to make the corrections you made in their final paper (while complaining the whole time about how tedious it is to teach writing). This is the drill sergeant version of teaching writing.

I would rather that you picture yourself as an orchestra conductor—you provide practice time, offering specific feedback periodically, letting groups of similar musicians work together to solve issues. The conductor does not, ever, run around and try to play each instrument.

What we have learned from these restrictive environments is that students rarely grow as writers (Kittle, 2008; Lane, 1993). They get used to relying on the teacher to "fix" their paper. It is one of the issues that college instructors point to in remedial writing courses—students haven't learned the skills necessary to revise, edit, and proofread their own papers. We may use scaffolding when it comes to the teaching of minilessons in Guided Writing, but we have yet to hand over the responsibility of writing (Fisher, 2006). Set a goal to create independent writers.

Instructional Practices to Update

Updated Strategy #1: Implement the Focused Question Card Strategy to Make Peer Revision Meaningful

Let's put it out there: Traditional peer editing does not work. This is what happens—students trade papers. They correct things that they don't really know how to correct and then hand the paper back to their partner. You lost instructional time, and they gained almost nothing valuable to add to their paper.

If we have the goal of creating independent writers, we have to teach students how to use a peer effectively for both revision and editing. Alexa Sandmann (2006) created a strategy to make peer revision and editing meaningful and purposeful with students of all ages. Here are the steps for implementation:

1. Convene a conversation between the writer and their text. After a minilesson is taught and students have had time to apply the technique to their own writing is a perfect time to have students think about the effectiveness of their writing. Other times to use this strategy are on a Friday, after a number of minilessons have been taught during Guided Writing, and prior to submission of a completed piece. Students need to think about what clarifications they need to make their text better. For example, if a minilesson on sensory language had been taught, they could ask themselves, "Does my use of sensory language make my writing come alive for my reader? How so?" After a minilesson on

introductions, writers could ask themselves, "Is my introduction engaging enough? Does it make a reader want to read more?" Start a list of these revising questions with your students, making some minilesson-specific and others more general to the writing process. Table 6.1 contains a list of possible revision questions for students to borrow and adapt. Students write their revising question on a note card.

2. Once students have defined and selected a revising question, they partner up. Sandmann (2006) suggests students choose their partner for this process. The first student hands his or her note card to the partner. They talk briefly about the question, going deeper into the needs of the writer, if necessary.

3. The first student reads his or her paper aloud to the partner. Partners sit across from each other, preventing the listener from making any edits to the paper. Under no circumstances do students surrender control of their paper to their partner. This accomplishes a few things: The student reading gets the benefit of watching their partner react to their text, achieving what Murray calls the complete act of writing (1987). It also allows students to use their ear as an editor (Murray, 1987). As any good writer will tell you, reading a text aloud allows you to catch all kinds of editing issues. Even though we are using this strategy as a revision strategy first, reading aloud helps students pay attention to editing issues, too!

4. The listener pays attention to the paper, using the focused question card as the guide. If time is an issue, what is read aloud can be only the portion that pertains to the revising question (e.g., if the question is about the introduction, only read the introduction!).

5. Partners discuss the answer to the focused question. The listener then summarizes the conversation on the note card and returns it to his or her partner.

6. Students switch roles, switch cards, and begin again.

This strategy is a hit for so many reasons. Students learn to identify questions they need to answer about their drafts. Students learn how to read aloud to edit their writing. Students learn to use a peer for effective revision. It's a win-win-win situation!

On the teacher side of things, this strategy helps alleviate the need to conference with every single student every single day (which is truly not possible). You are moving students to a place of independence where they begin to rely on a peer and themselves to strengthen their writing.

Table 6.1 Possible Revision Questions for the Focused Question Card Strategy

1. Does the ending come too abruptly?
2. Do I confuse the reader?
3. Should I add more detail? Where?
4. Did I keep the same point of view?
5. Did my final paragraph continue with the main idea of the story?
6. Does my introduction set the stage for the rest of my writing?
7. Does my concluding paragraph wrap up the main thoughts of my writing?
8. Is my writer's voice coming through? How?
9. Did the extra background about _____ help my story? Or did it seem like too much?
10. Are the examples appropriate and in the right place?
11. Should/could my introduction be more positive?
12. Is the conclusion effective enough?
13. Is there a flow to the memory?
14. Does the beginning make sense and draw you in? Does my ending provide a good stopping point?
15. Should I rewrite my introduction?
16. Do I need a better conclusion?
17. Do my beginning and title fit?
18. Does the part about saying _____ seem too rushed? Does it need more?
19. Does the language help bring my personal experiences/memories alive for the reader? Can you visualize _____?
20. What suggestions do you have for the final passage in my introduction?
21. Should there be a specific order to how I present _____?
22. My piece revolves around several _____. Would the word _____ be a better choice?
23. Does the conclusion conclude?
24. Is my ending too melodramatic?

Source: Sandmann, 2006.

When I first tried out this strategy, I was very specific about what revising issue that my students would address with their partner. If I had taught a minilesson, our Focused Question Card conferences were about that minilesson technique. As my students got more proficient in the strategy, I felt better about allowing students to choose their own questions and revision issues to address. In fact, students begin to use this strategy on their own, organically: Students would finish something with their draft. Rather than waiting on me to conference with them, they would go to what they called the FQC (for

Focused Question Card) corner. They would work on their note card, defining their revising question. And they would wait for a partner to join them. It was a joy to behold!

A final word on the Focused Question Card strategy: It can be used for editing conferences, too. Create a list of editing issues. Have students choose one and write it on a note card. This time during the strategy, students sit next to each other, although the writer still retains control of his or her paper. The paper is still read aloud. The listener is allowed to point out changes that relate to the editing issue, but only the writer can add them to the paper.

Updated Strategy #2: Embed Language Instruction (Grammar and Mechanics) Into Guided Writing Through Effective Minilessons

"That workbook page really showed me how to use commas effectively," said no student ever. What that workbook page did was assess if a student knows how to use commas correctly. Workbooks and other skill-and-drill activities do not teach a student a skill (Allington, 2002); they assess that skill. Hillocks and Smith have even made the statement that "research over a period of nearly 90 years has consistently shown that teaching of school grammar has little or no effect on students' writing" (Hillocks & Smith, 1991, p. 602). However, teachers go back to this kind of instruction because they do not have a better alternative (Folz-Gray, 2012).

Embedded language instruction is the best way to help students learn the skills they need to communicate effectively (Jones, Myhill, & Bailey, 2013). Mechanics and grammar are both written communication skills that need to be taught in the context of the student's writing, just like elements of each genre need to be taught and applied to student writing.

The best strategies that I can show you are minilessons you can use in your classroom. These minilessons should be rooted in Guided Writing, taught in the midst of revision lessons. All these lessons would be applied to a student draft, making language instruction meaningful and purposeful (Lane, 1993).

Language Minilesson #3: Spelling

Rather than offer a traditional spelling minilesson, I will offer a set of tips to move students forward with spelling at the intermediate, middle, and high school levels. There is no lesson that is a magic wand with spelling for older students—we instead need to develop what I call their "spelling sense." Spelling sense is like Spidey Sense in the Spiderman movies—Spiderman just *knows* when trouble exists in the same way that a writer *knows* that a word is spelled wrong. You have invoked your spelling sense standing in

Figure 6.1   Language Minilesson #1: Verb Tenses

Unit/Genre: *Applicable to any genre but works well with narrative* **Complete standard:** *Use verb tense to convey various times, sequences, states, and conditions.* **Portion of the standard for emphasis in this lesson:** *Same*

Modeling:

1. Choose an item from your Heart Map or Neighborhood Map (see chapter 8) and write a story about a specific event.

2. Explain to students that for a story to have full impact, a verb tense needs to be consistent. Introduce a verb tense anchor chart. Write present, future, and past on the anchor chart.

3. Have students look through independent reading books or the class library and identify the tense of a variety of books. On the chart, write verbs that show a specific tense that students find.

4. Return to your model story. Have students identify what tense you are writing in. Model changing your verb tense to another tense to stay consistent and for impact.

Guided Practice:

1. Distribute sample paragraphs to groups of students. Have students work together to practice amending the verb tense to a different tense. Let students discuss which tense has the most impact.

2. Formative assessment: Have students share with the class the original and amended paragraphs. Check to see that verbs are changed consistently to the target verb tense, as chosen by the students. Keep note of students who struggle with this concept.

Directions for Independent Practice:

1. Direct students to look at their current draft. Using the anchor chart, ask students to consider what tense they are writing their story in. Then have them check their verb tense for consistency and impact.

2. Focused Question Card strategy time! Use the editing question "Is my verb tense consistent? I am writing in the _____ tense." Have students partner up and listen to check for consistent verb tense.

Reteaching ideas:

1. Have students work to take apart sample paragraphs into the three different tenses as shown on the anchor chart.

2. Assist students in identifying the tense the want to write in for their personal drafts. Help each student set a goal in checking verb tense in their own drafts.

Figure 6.2 Language Minilesson #2: Sentence Variation

Unit/Genre: *Applicable to any genre*
Complete standard: *Choose among simple, compound, complex, and compound-complex sentences to signal differing relationships among ideas.*
Portion of the standard for emphasis in this lesson: *Same*

Modeling:

1. Display a piece of effective writing for students to read (Figure 8.2 in chapter 8 works well).

2. Read the piece aloud to students, asking them to comment about what they appreciate about the writing.

3. Point out the author's use of sentence variation. Introduce an anchor chart on sentence variation. Write simple, compound, and complex sentences on the anchor chart. Help students define each type of sentence.

4. Use the sample writing to identify each type of sentence. Discuss the impact of each sentence on the overall work.

5. Model for students how to take a simple sentence and turn it into either a compound or a complex sentence. Discuss how the passage changes by doing so (if using Figure 8.2, you could change the sentence that reads, "She got really nervous and turned pale and literally broke into a sweat within a minute, and then she came up with some lame excuse about really having to go to the bathroom," into several simple sentences).

Guided Practice:

1. Place a variety of books on each table group. Ask students to skim through writing, finding sentences that fit into each type of sentence.

2. Have students write each type of sentence on a sentence strip to collect for display under the anchor chart.

Directions for Independent Practice:

1. Direct students to look at their current draft. Using the anchor chart and displayed sentences, ask students to consider their sentence variety.

2. Ask students to set a personal goal for sentence variety. How many different types of each sentence do they think will be optimal for their particular draft?

3. Give each student a sticky note to write their goal.

4. Have students work on their drafts to meet their sentence variety goal.

Reteaching ideas:

1. Work with small groups of students to identify the types of sentences they use most in their writing.

2. Help individual students set a goal to increase their sentence variety. Highlight sentences that could be combined to make compound or complex sentences.

front of your classroom: You are writing something on the board or typing something on the overhead and you write a word. It just doesn't look right. You start to sweat a little, worried that someone will notice. That is your spelling sense kicking in. We need students to develop a spelling sense, and that is something that we can't teach through spelling lists! Instead, create a poster or anchor chart, sharing these tips:

Spelling tip #1: If students write a word that they are unsure of the spelling, have them take a sticky note and write it three different ways. When they meet with a partner or confer with you, they can bring that sticky note and get a second opinion. They can also use that to help them in using a dictionary to correct spelling.

Spelling tip #2: Read aloud. We already went over this using the Focused Question Card strategy, but one of the best ways to catch misspellings is to read your text aloud. You do not have to wait for a partner to read to, either; simply take your draft somewhere and read it aloud. Mark the words that you think may be spelled incorrectly.

Spelling tip #3: Befriend a good speller. There is a reason why people have jobs like proofreader and editor; they have a grasp of the English language that others lack. Chances are, you have students in your room with strong skills in these areas. This is one of the few times I condone students trading papers. If there is a student who is an excellent speller who doesn't mind helping peers out with spelling, let them help out their friends (and you!) by proofreading.

Spelling tip #4: Use the tools available to you. We may assume that students know how to use the spell check feature on the computer—DON'T. Remind students to use electronic tools to improve a paper; it is the way of the world!

Common Core Connection

The strategies shared in this chapter match well with the revision and editing standards included in the writing standards (see Table 6.2).

Table 6.2 Revision and Editing Standards

Grade Level	4	5	6
Standard Addressed	**Writing** With guidance and support from peers and adults, develop and strengthen writing as needed by planning, revising, and editing.	**Writing** With guidance and support from peers and adults, develop and strengthen writing as needed by planning, revising, editing, rewriting, or trying a new approach.	**Writing** With some guidance and support from peers and adults, develop and strengthen writing as needed by planning, revising, editing, rewriting, or trying a new approach.
	7	**8**	**9–10**
	Writing With some guidance and support from peers and adults, develop and strengthen writing as needed by planning, revising, editing, rewriting, or trying a new approach, focusing on how well purpose and audience have been addressed.	**Writing** With some guidance and support from peers and adults, develop and strengthen writing as needed by planning, revising, editing, rewriting, or trying a new approach, focusing on how well purpose and audience have been addressed.	**Writing** Develop and strengthen writing as needed by planning, revising, editing, rewriting, or trying a new approach, focusing on addressing what is most significant for a specific purpose and audience.

Action Steps

Creating opportunities to revise and edit with purpose and meaning is central to establishing a writing process in your classroom. It is time to take some action . . .

1. Do you feel cautious or confident in implementing the Focused Question Card strategy with your students? Why?

   _____

   _____

2. Make a plan for using the Focused Question Card strategy in your class-room. Could you see yourself implementing it after specific minilessons? Identify them. Do you see yourself using it after a set of minilessons? Which ones? Or do you see yourself reserving this strategy for after all Guided Writing lessons have taken place to help polish final drafts?

   _____

   _____

3. How do you feel about replacing skill and drill language lessons with authentic writing minilessons, embedded in Guided Writing? What frightens you about this idea? What delights you about this idea?

   _____

   _____

Works Cited

Allington, R. (2002). What I've learned about effective reading instruction: From a decade of studying exemplary elementary classroom teacher. *Phi Delta Kappan, 83,* 740–747.

Fisher, R. (2006). Whose writing is it anyways? Issues of control of the teaching of writing. *Cambridge Journal of Education, 36,* 193–206.

Folz-Gray, D. (2012). Response to error: Sentence-level error and the teacher of basic writing. *Research and Teaching in Developmental Writing, 28,* 18–29.

Hillocks, G., & Smith, M. (1991). Grammar and usage. In J. Flood, J.M. Jensen, D. Lapp, & J.R. Squire (Eds.), *Handbook of research on teaching the English language arts* (pp. 591–603). New York: MacMillan.

Jones, S., Myhill, D., & Bailey, T. (2013). Grammar for writing? An investigation on the effects of contextualized grammar teaching on students' writing. *Reading & Writing, 26,* 1241–1263.

Kittle, P. (2008). *Write beside them: Risk, voice, and clarity in high school writing*. Portsmouth, NH: Heinemann.

Lane, B. (1993). *After the end: Teaching and learning creative revision*. Portsmouth, NH: Heinemann.

Murray, D. (1987). *Write to learn* (2nd ed.). New York: Holt, Rinehart & Winston.

Sandmann, A. (2006). Nurturing thoughtful revision using the Focused Question Card strategy. *Journal of Adolescent and Adult Literacy, 50*, 20–28.

Zumbrunn, S., & Krause, K. (2012). Conversations with leaders: Principles of effective writing instruction. *Reading Teacher, 65*, 346–353.

Chapter 7

Use Conferencing to Grow Students as Thoughtful, Reflective Writers

Janine got up from our conference looking a little disoriented. "Aren't you gonna correct something on my paper?" I laughed and then grew serious when I saw the concerned look on her face. "No, Janine. Do you know what you are going to do when you leave here to work on your paper?" "Yeah," she said, referencing the sticky note in her hand. "I'm going to look at the transition word reference sheet you gave us and pick four more transition words to use in my paper. I will then check through each paragraph to see if transition words would help them flow, too." She looked up. "I just thought this would be a little more painful, that's all."

Why Is This Item on the List So Important?

Conferencing is the most mystifying topic in Writers' Workshop. In fact, when I teach a professional development session on Writers' Workshop, I often call conferencing the advanced version of workshop teaching: I advise teachers to master the minilessons first and then move onto the conferencing. Yet, it is conferencing that distinguishes Writers' Workshop from teaching the basic writing process; it is the time when we get to meet writers at their ability level and grow them individually as writers. And it's a beautiful thing.

Conferencing was conceived as the time to give feedback that matters to students (Atwell, 1987; Kittle, 2008). Students do not have to worry about whether their piece is off-base; they are secure that their teacher will check in with them several times throughout the writing process to help point them in the right direction. The key is to make conferences manageable for the teacher and focused enough for the student that each leaves conferencing time feeling that the time used was valuable to both parties.

> **Do this—not that principle #7**: DO use conferencing to grow students as thoughtful, reflective writers. DON'T use conferencing to edit or correct papers, with a scattered focus.

To Get Started

Conferencing is scary because it requires the one thing that I can't give you: time. You need time to be able to conference with your students about their papers. One of the reasons why I favor the unit planner where you teach a minilesson one day and then have students apply the minilesson on a second day is because that automatically gives you time to meet with students to conference about their papers (see chapter 1).

There are a few practices that bear sharing to make conferencing feasible in your classroom:

♦ *Allow the student to retain ownership of the paper and take the lead of the writing conference.* Just as in the anecdote that started this chapter, students are conditioned to believe that teachers exist to "fix" their papers. When I conduct a writing conference, I try to sit across from students, just like in the Focused Question Card strategy shared in chapter 6. This prevents my itchy English teacher fingers from editing their paper.

♦ *Find one focus and stick to it.* It is so easy to want to cover a million and one things in a writing conference. I like to begin the conference by asking the student if he or she feels comfortable with the most recently taught minilesson, a great starting place for a singular focus. If the student does feel comfortable and confident (and I might have them read me a sentence or paragraph proving their efficacy), I will then ask what he or she wants to focus on. This leads to the next bullet . . .

♦ *Students should know what they want to focus on.* Writing conferences should not be a surprise; they should be an accepted practice in the writing classroom as a time to receive feedback on a paper. So students should keep a running list of questions they want answered. Teaching the Focused Question Card strategy helps with this so much—students already know how to define revision issues and write a question that addresses them. I even know teachers that require students to bring a note card with them to a conference with a revision question written on it to provide instant focus.

♦ *Have a visible signal to let students know that you are occupied.* I don't care whether your students are 8 or 18; they will find a reason to interrupt your writing conferences. I found that the only way to combat this issue was to first talk about it with students. I wanted them to know how much I value conferencing time and that I hoped that they would learn to value it, too. My statement usually went something like this: "Writers, when conferencing time begins, give me the time and space to meet with each of you to discuss your writing. If you are bleeding or about to have an accident, then, and only then, are you allowed to interrupt me." I then showed my signal. I wore a Princess Aurora (from Sleeping Beauty) tiara to signal to students that I was conferencing and therefore should not be interrupted. If the tiara was on my head, they knew to find their own answers until it was removed. Other signals I have seen (and celebrated) are an artist smock (to up the "workshop" idea), a chef's hat (because ideas are cooking), a magician's hat (because magic is in the making!), and a traffic light signal (red means no interruptions!). Decide on a signal, introduce it to students, and use it!

♦ *Go to students rather than them coming to you.* This is an idea I borrowed from Nancie Atwell's book *The Reading Zone* (2007). She described conferencing with her students during Reading Workshop as a time for her to enter into the student's space to discuss reading. I liked that but also thought of it in practical terms; when you call a student up to your desk (or lair, considering how so many teachers have built desk fortresses to protect their corner of the classroom), you are opening up an opportunity for them to touch, bother, and talk to every kid between their desk and your desk. And, let's face it—preteens and teenagers are generally not the most graceful bunch. Go to the students to conference; it is the best way to provide the least interruption to students.

♦ *But don't kneel next to desks.* Okay, this is a personal pet peeve. And when I tell you the origins of this story, you will laugh. I had a very unhappy cat once. Getting him to the vet was torture. On one unfortunate visit, he was hissing and spitting on the examination table when the vet entered. She immediately dropped to her knees, much to the astonishment of my husband and me. She whispered, "I'm letting the cat establish his dominance" (by the way, he had feline AIDS and was probably in pain most of his sad, short life). From then on, any time I saw a teacher on his or her knees, conferencing with a student, I couldn't help but picture that vet. You don't need to allow students to establish their dominance. Instead, use a chair so you can sit as equals during a conference.

♦ *No ducklings.* If students DO have a question while you are conferencing, I do not encourage them to line up at the desk you are working at, waiting for you to be done to ask you a question. Set your conferencing routine to include that students will remain seated or working during writing time rather than lining up to ask you a question. I do not want them lined up like little ducklings, following the mother duck around!

♦ *The actionable item.* The true key to great conferences, in my opinion, is that students leave the conference with an action plan in hand. My favorite conferencing tools are sticky notes and a pen. As we talk, we create a plan for what the student can accomplish next. I write that plan on the sticky notes, a concrete reminder of where they should go next as a writer. I find that it is not enough to just chat with students and then move on to the next student; more often than not, that leads to a duckling waiting for me to ask, "What was I supposed to do again?" Leaving them with a piece of evidence to remind them how to proceed documents the process for both of us.

♦ *Keeping notes on conferencing.* There is no perfect management system for documenting your conferences. Instead you have to figure out which one works best for you *and* which system you will actually stick with. Here are a few ideas from master conferencers I know:

  ♦ *Dated rosters.* My friend Casey keeps multiple copies of her roster in a clipboard with a storage compartment. When she finds herself with time to conference, she pulls out a fresh list, dates it, and then makes quick notes on the roster on what she talked about with each student.

  ♦ *Conferencing sheet per student.* Lisa takes a slightly different approach: She has a clipboard with one piece of paper for each student. As she conferences, she flips to that student's page and documents the conversation, including what standard that she addressed.

♦ *GoogleDocs.* Brenda, a techie, has a GoogleDocs document that she can update from anywhere, without lugging her laptop around. She logs in from her smartphone or tablet, puts in a few notes for each student, along with the date, and moves on.

Instructional Practices to Update

Updated Strategy #1: Using a Schedule or the Golden Gate Method to Make Conferencing Happen as Much as Possible

There is a an article by Sarah J. Brooks (2006) that talks about how much she hates Nancie Atwell. Before you throw your hands up in disgust, find the article and read it; it is not about how much she dislikes Nancie but really about how you have to read what the experts tell us about a topic (like Writers' Workshop) and then make it your own. Conferencing is one of those topics. There are some fabulous books out there that address conferencing. Table 7.1 lists a few of my favorites, the ones that I consulted when I first started conferencing with my students during Writers' Workshop.

However, even after consulting these experts, I found that there is really only one way to start conferencing with students: Whatever way you will actually stick with. Don't groan! Conferencing is very personal. Your teaching style will dictate how conferencing goes in your room.

Approaching conferencing as a mathematical problem. My first conferencing iteration involved a two-week schedule. I took each class roster and figured out how many students I could see each day if I conferenced for 5 minutes per student. I typically had 30 students in a class so I felt that it was attainable for me to conference with three students a day, for a total of 15 minutes. I posted the schedule so that students could see exactly when I would meet them over the two-week period. I set a timer so I wouldn't go over the time. Table 7.2 shows the pros and cons of using a schedule to make conferencing happen in your classroom.

Table 7.1   Expert Advice on Conferencing in Writers' Workshop

1. *One to one: The art of conferring with young writers,* Lucy Calkins (2005).
2. *How's it going?: A practical guide to conferring with student writers,* Carl Anderson (2000).
3. *So what do they really know?: Assessment that informs teaching and learning* Cris Tovani (2011).

Table 7.2 The Pros and Cons of Using a Schedule for Writing Conferences

PROS	CONS
1. Students knew exactly when they got to meet with me so they weren't constantly asking me for a conference. 2. I felt confident that I was conferencing with my students regularly. 3. I had 5 minutes with each student, every conference.	1. I may have missed some conferences with students who needed me earlier, not on a schedule. 2. I was conferencing with students who didn't necessarily need to talk at that time. 3. There were times when I didn't need 5 minutes to cover what was necessary. There were times when I needed more than 5 minutes, too.

Using the Golden Gate method of conferencing. Donalyn Miller is the brilliant creator of this method of conferencing (2014). She begins by telling the story of the Golden Gate Bridge: The bridge is in a constant state of rusting. To combat this condition, brought on by the ocean winds and Bay Area rains, a crew is painting the Golden Gate Bridge at all times. And when they finish, they simply start all over again.

Painting the Golden Gate Bridge is a perfect analogy for conferencing. You do the best you can, conferencing with as many students as possible. You conference with who needs you at that moment, using formative assessment to help you prioritize. And when you make it through all of your students, maybe in two days, maybe in five, maybe in a few weeks, you start all over again.

For those of you who are ready to break free of a restrictive conferencing schedule, the Golden Gate method may be right for you. It helps you clarify quality over quantity when it comes to conferencing (Glasswell, Parr & McNaughton, 2003).

Updated Strategy #2: Go Beyond One-on-One Conferences to Reach a Broader Audience and Motivate Students as Writers

One-on-one conferences are great as formative assessments and for personalizing content for individual students. But there are other types of conferences that are just as appropriate to use during Guided Writing that help you reach a broader audience for a variety of purposes:

- ◆ *Compliment "conferences."* More than anything else, struggling and reluctant writers need to be encouraged to write. I use a compliment conference as a time to offer students specific praise to motivate them in their writing process. This can be as simple as walking around, reading over shoulders, and writing a positive comment on a sticky note for students to read. Students *cherish* these sticky notes (as well as compare their note with their neighbor's note, so make sure you personalize comments for each student). If you want to make it more formal, keep a record of ways that you can compliment the student's writing after a few individual conferences to make it more meaningful (Fountas & Pinell, 2000).

♦ *Group conferences.* Teaching points can be the same for multiple students. I figure this out by doing a status walk of student writing: Maybe I flip through notebooks the night before or maybe I walk around the class at the beginning of independent practice. In either case, I keep a note of whom I could conference with as a team. The conference goes the same—students read aloud to me, we discuss a focus point, and they leave with an actionable item—but I am able to get to more students by using this technique periodically.

Common Core Connection

The strategies presented in this chapter meet the revision and editing standards presented in the writing standards of the Common Core State Standards (see Table 7.3).

Table 7.3   Revision and Editing Standards

Grade Level	4	5	6
Standard Addressed	**Writing** With guidance and support from peers and adults, develop and strengthen writing as needed by planning, revising, and editing.	**Writing** With guidance and support from peers and adults, develop and strengthen writing as needed by planning, revising, editing, rewriting, or trying a new approach.	**Writing** With some guidance and support from peers and adults, develop and strengthen writing as needed by planning, revising, editing, rewriting, or trying a new approach.

(Continued)

Table 7.3 Continued

	7	8	9–10
	Writing With some guidance and support from peers and adults, develop and strengthen writing as needed by planning, revising, editing, rewriting, or trying a new approach, focusing on how well purpose and audience have been addressed.	**Writing** With some guidance and support from peers and adults, develop and strengthen writing as needed by planning, revising, editing, rewriting, or trying a new approach, focusing on how well purpose and audience have been addressed.	**Writing** Develop and strengthen writing as needed by planning, revising, editing, rewriting, or trying a new approach, focusing on addressing what is most significant for a specific purpose and audience.

Action Steps

Conferencing is not easy, but it is worth the time and effort to watch your students blossom as writers under your tutelage. It is time to take some action . . .

1. After reading this chapter, what is still holding you back from conferencing regularly with your students?

   _____

   _____

2. What do you think your "do not interrupt" signal will be? Be creative!

   _____

   _____

3. Do you think you will develop a conferencing schedule or go with the "Golden Gate" method? Why?

_____

_____

4. Think of two similar students in your room, writing-wise. What could be the focal point of a group conference with these two students?

_____

_____

Works Cited

Anderson, C. (2000). *How's it going: A practical guide to conferring with student writers.* Portsmouth, NH: Heinemann.

Atwell, N. (1987). *In the middle: New understandings about writing, reading, and learning.* Portsmouth, NH: Heinemann.

Atwell, N. (2007). *The reading zone: How to help kids become skilled, passionate, habitual, critical readers.* New York: Scholastic.

Brooks, S. (2006). New voices: Why I detest Nancie Atwell. *English Journal, 95,* 92–95.

Calkins, L. (2005). *One to one: The art of conferring with young writers.* Portsmouth, NH: Heinemann.

Fountas, I., & Pinell, G. (2000). *Guiding readers and writers: Teaching comprehension, genre, and content literacy.* Portsmouth, NH: Heinemann.

Glasswell, K., Parr, M., & McNaughton, S. (2003). Four ways to work against yourself when conferencing with struggling writers. *Language Arts, 80,* 291–298.

Kittle, P. (2008). *Write beside them: Risk, voice, and clarity in high school writing.* Portsmouth, NH: Heinemann.

Miller, D. (2014). *Conferring with readers to find focus.* Paper delivered at the Kent State Literacy Conference, Kent, Ohio, October 31.

Tovani, C. (2011). *So what do they really know?: Assessment that informs teaching and learning.* Boston: Stenhouse.

Chapter 8

Let Narratives Be Personal and Creative, Focusing on Details and Imagery to Make a Story Come to Life

My students in East Los Angeles were reluctant to write on topics that I thought were interesting: What did they want to be when they grow up? Who did they look up to? What did they do over the weekend? In my narrow, suburban mind, I thought they simply didn't have enough experiences to write a lot to these prompts, but I persisted, certain that one of them would encourage writing. I finally stumbled on a narrative prompt that got them writing—we had just read a nonfiction story about the Titanic. My students were fascinated by the stories of people using the famous ship to immigrate to the United States. "That sure is different than how my family came to the U.S., Miss," Dulcie remarked. "How did your family get here?" I asked. A thousand hands shot up. "Do you all have stories about this?" I inquired. Heads nodded vigorously. "Take out a piece of paper," I instructed, inspired. For once, no one complained. "Tell me your immigration stories." You could have heard a pin drop. It was the best writing that I got all year.

Why Is This Item on the List So Important?

Narrative writing was conceived as pushback to the formulaic writing that had been taught in schools for decades (Johnson, 2014). Teachers began to work to honor student voice, and luminaries such as Nancie Atwell (1998) encouraged teachers to help students find the stories locked within them through personal narratives. My students in the anecdote had amazing stories to tell, but I had to be willing to listen. They needed more than superficial (and finite!) prompts to unlock the writer within.

Narrative reading and writing are at the heart of the human condition. Our ancestors were storytellers, and that need to tell and hear stories is in our DNA. This was so apparent as my students read and discussed their immigration stories—my students' families had to fight to live in Los Angeles, whether it meant smuggling a baby by using a borrowed passport or paying a "coyote" to sneak a family over the border under the light of the moon. It opened my eyes to who they were as individuals, more than any "What is your favorite . . ." prompt would ever do.

> Do this—not that principle #8: DO let narratives be personal and creative, focusing on details and imagery to make a story come to life. DON'T limit narrative writing to "One time . . ." stories.

To Get Started

The place of narrative writing in the English/Language Arts curriculum has been debated with the advent of the Common Core State Standards. The anchor standard itself begins, "Write narratives to develop real or imagined events" (CCSS, 2010). Teachers happily assumed that this meant that their personal narrative or memoir units were safe. Then the assessments that would eventually measure growth on these standards were released, and it looked like students would not be asked to write a personal narrative but instead be asked to write a piece of creative fiction based on a piece of text. What is a teacher to do?

The case for personal narratives. Personal narratives still have a place in the ELA classroom. To teach students how to write excellent stories, it is always helpful to start with the person that matters to students most—themselves!

Story structure, sensory details, dialogue—all the elements of excellent narratives can be taught and applied to personal narratives.

The shift that I see in the Common Core State Standards is that your narrative writing unit cannot begin and end with personal narratives. Keep personal narratives in your classroom, but let that be only half of your narrative writing instruction. Devote the other half to creative fiction, allowing students to apply all they have learned about structuring excellent stories from your personal narrative unit to stories that they create.

Teachers often shy away from having students write creative fiction beyond the occasional Halloween scary story. They fear that students won't have enough ideas and will struggle to write. Donalyn Miller talks about underground readers in *The Book Whisperer* (2009); there are underground writers in your classroom, too! And the kinds of writing they are doing on the side? Creative fiction! Bring these students above ground by legitimizing creative fiction in your classroom.

Instructional Practices to Update

Updated Strategy #1: Using Heart Mapping or Neighborhood Mapping to Mine Students' Experiences and Lives for Writing Ideas

There are some writing strategies that are so great that they deserve top billing in classrooms. Both Heart Mapping and Neighborhood Mapping fall into that category. Used as an introductory activity to begin a narrative writing unit, either strategy will provide a wealth of stories for your students to tell. Both prevent what I call Narrative Summary Syndrome. Narrative Summary Syndrome is when students write about an experience, but rather than writing deeply about a small moment, they summarize this experience in a maddeningly passive tone. I live close to a major amusement park called Cedar Point, and it is an event in children's lives in northeast Ohio to go during summer vacations. I have gotten a plethora of paragraphs about this trip to Cedar Point written under Narrative Summary Syndrome that generally go something like this:

> I went to Cedar Point. It was fun. We rode a lot of roller coasters.
> I ate a hot dog. We played games. I can't wait to go again.

Heart Mapping. Georgia Heard first wrote about Heart Mapping in her book, *Awakening the Heart: Exploring Poetry in Elementary and Middle School*

(1998). Here are the steps necessary for implementing this strategy in your classroom:

1. Display a Heart Map template (Figure 8.1) enlarged for your students to view. If you feel that the template may limit student responses, use a blank heart instead of the divided heart pictured in this chapter.

2. At the center of the heart, put the most important person, place, or thing to you. Work your way through the other spaces in your heart. Think aloud as you place ideas in each section. Be specific! Don't just say "My cat, Tosca"; say, "My cat, Tosca, who we bought at PetSmart during an adoption event," and write, "Adopting Tosca at PetSmart."

3. Distribute a Heart Map to each student. Encourage students to fill in each section, considering how to address the most important people, places, and things in their lives. Give time for this; allow students to reflect and think deeply as they fill out the template. Heard also encourages students to color code their heart, if they wish: People they care about could be colored a specific color, events another color, and places a third color (Heard, 1998).

4. Turn and talk: Give students time to discuss and share their Heart Map with a partner. Model telling a very specific story from your Heart Map. I always use frozen M&Ms to model this part of the strategy: I first tell a Narrative Summary Syndrome story about M&Ms that sounds like this:

   > I like M&Ms. They are my favorite candy. I am excited when I get them for Halloween. The blue and green colors are my favorites.
   > I then tell a Heart Map story that sounds like this:
   > > Frozen M&Ms are truly the only way to eat M&Ms. I found this out one year trick-or-treating. My mom confiscated all of my candy and hid it. I despaired until I realized where she hid it—in the freezer! Every day, I would sneak one piece of deeply frozen candy out of the freezer and savor it in the privacy of my bedroom. It was then I discovered the perfection that is frozen M&Ms. They last longer because you have to melt them in your mouth so as to not break a tooth. The candy taste lingers just right in your mouth. It is heaven on earth!

5. For the rest of the personal narrative portion of your narrative writing unit, encourage students to use their Heart Maps to find specific stories to tell.

Figure 8.1   Heart Mapping Template

My Heart Map

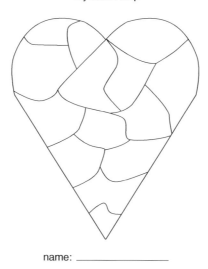

name: _____

Neighborhood Mapping. In *Knots in My Yo-Yo String*, Jerry Spinelli's fabulous boyhood memoir, the book opens with a detailed illustration of the small town where the author grew up (1998). Special places like the baseball field and park are labeled. Houses the family lived in are scattered around the page. The places where special events took place are drawn in with arrows. Before we read a word of Jerry's prose, we are immediately pulled into his world through a neighborhood map.

Ralph Fletcher formalized using this strategy to spur memoir writing in his book, *How to Write Your Life Story* (2007). Like Heart Mapping, it invites students to mine their personal experiences for writing ideas; unlike Heart Mapping, it places them in a very specific context, the neighborhood in which they live. I have tried this with students in a rural area (who mostly drew their farms), an urban area (where apartment buildings were sketched), and the 'burbs—they all work. Here are the steps for implementing this strategy in your classroom:

1. On a blank piece of paper in front of the class, model for students drawing a neighborhood where you lived while growing up. Start basic (streets and landmarks) and then begin to add stories. For example, on my map, I could draw the mountains across the street from our house that caught fire every summer because of drought. I would add the path that ran behind our street, where I played with my best friend Megan every afternoon. And I would add stick

figures on the street next to mine to show how all the neighborhood kids played Kick the Can on warm spring nights until our parents called us in (I just dated myself, didn't I?).

2. Ask students to pick a "story" from your map. Begin to write out the narrative connected to this picture, modeling how these memories make for perfect memoir stories.

3. Distribute blank paper to students (11 × 14 works best if you can find it!). Encourage students to begin to draw either the neighborhood where they live currently or a favorite neighborhood from the past.

4. As students work, remind students to add detail via the stories that occurred around their neighborhood. Stories about neighbors, important milestones, scary stories—all of these can be included on the neighborhood map.

5. Pair students up and have them take their partner on a virtual walk through their chosen neighborhood. Urge students to tell one specific story that is inspired by their map to their partner.

6. Writing time! Allow students to begin drafting that one special story. The basis for a memoir has begun!

One thing that I am sensitive to with neighborhood mapping is students who are in the foster care system or who lack secure housing. An activity like this would be cruel to a student who doesn't experience a stable housing situation. This is why I offer both Heart Mapping and Neighborhood Mapping. Choose the one that best suits your students' needs.

Updated Strategy #2: Using Story Starters and Fiction Texts to Spur the Writing of Creative Fiction

People have a love/hate relationship with creative writing. We never "kind of like" creative writing; we are either writing stories under our blankets at night with a flashlight or we are groaning audibly when assigned a creative writing piece in class. This means that teachers have to walk a fine line. I don't want to stifle the creativity of those who are already in love with creative writing, but I have to find a way to encourage my reluctant writers.

Story starters as Everyday Writing prompts. Writing without inspiration can be scary for a reluctant writer. This why story starters work so well; they plunge the writer into a plot, allowing them to hang their creative hat on an idea that they can develop. Story starters are also an easy way to break the five-paragraph essay habit of students and teachers. It is hard for a great story to fit into a five-paragraph essay mold. Students instead are able to consider conflict, characters, and setting, all elements often provided by the story starter, around which to build a story.

Story starter resources proliferate on the Internet. Table 8.1 lists a few of my favorite electronic resources for traditional story starters and story starter generators.

Beyond traditional story starters, pictures provide excellent possibilities for creative writing opportunities. My colleague Jeff uses this strategy every summer while facilitating the National Writing Project Summer Institute at Kent State University: He posts a variety of historical and obscure photos around the room and invites students to wander, observe the photos, and ponder the stories behind them. We then return to our seats and write, imagining the narratives behind the pictures. Just like with a traditional story starter, the pictures provide characters, setting, and often conflict.

Sequels, prequels, and alternative points of view. An easy fit into most language arts classrooms, assigning sequels, prequels, and stories telling an alternative point of view is an easy way to encourage creative writing in students. So much is provided when students use a shared story for the basis of something new: The characters have been developed. The setting has been fully established. The key to finding good stories to write a sequel are securing fiction texts with cliff-hangers that could lead to excellent "Part II" stories. Prequels are best linked to a story where a character or idea is not fully developed and the reader wants more. And any story can be rewritten from another character's point of view.

Table 8.1   Story Starter Websites

1.   www.scholastic.com/teachers/story-starters: This website delineates story starters by genre—adventure, fantasy, sci-fi, and "scrambler." Students will get all the essential elements to get writing with the pull of a lever (appropriate for grades 4–6).
2.   http://thestorystarter.com and www.thestorystarter.com/jr.htm: These sites provide students with one wildly creative sentence to get the juices flowing. Don't like what you got? Click the button to receive another prompt!
3.   www.literacyshed.com/the-story-starter-shed.html: This list of creative story starters was crowdsourced. Students are sure to find one crafty line to get a story started.

Published literature (and the movie industry) has been mining this field of sequels, prequels, and alternative points of view for years! One of my favorite young adult authors, James Howe, wrote *The Misfits* in 2001. It is about a group of quirky middle school students who forge a strong friendship. *The Misfits* focuses on Bobby. The sequels, *Totally Joe* (2005) and *Addie on the Inside* (2011), center on a different character featured in the original, a perfect example of alternative–point of view writing.

Content Area Connection

Although narratives are not listed as a genre to be specifically taught by content area teachers, I find that narratives can fit well into the content area classroom. Social Studies teachers, in particular, have been writing narratives to bring history to life for years. Retelling history from a first-person point of view, creating a character in order to place oneself into an important historical event, and using letter writing to explain historical actions can all work beautifully to translate content learning into meaningful writing experiences.

Sample minilesson: " 'It's like I'm there!' Teaching students how to identify and use sensory language to make narrative writing come alive."

As promised, here is a minilesson to use in conjunction with narrative writing.

Table 8.2   Narrative Writing Minilesson

Unit/Genre: Narrative Writing
Complete standard: *Use precise words and phrases, telling details, and sensory language to convey a vivid picture of the experiences, events, setting, and/or characters.* **Portion of the standard for emphasis in this lesson:** *Use sensory language to bring narrative writing to life.*
Modeling:
1. Display sample text for students to read (see Figure 8.2). 2. Read text aloud to students. 3. Ask students to pinpoint what makes this text so special. 4. Introduce teaching point on anchor chart. Ask students to turn to an elbow buddy or small group and discuss: How does sensory language make R. J. Palacio's writing special (30 seconds for discussion)?

5. Define sensory language with students. Add details to anchor chart that demonstrate the five senses.
6. Distribute handout titled "Sensory Language Wheel" (Figure 8.3) to students. Reread Palacio excerpt, pausing to chart sensory language on the chart as a class.
7. Model adding sensory language to the Palacio excerpt. For example, you could add the smell the powder made to the science portion of the chapter ("The powder smelled sharp as it melted on the aluminum foil").

Guided Practice:

1. In small groups, have students brainstorm at least two other ways that sensory language and details could be added to the Palacio excerpt (5–7 minutes, depending on proficiency of students).
2. Formative assessment: Have small groups share their additions. Students share the sensory language technique that they tried and then read their additions for the group. Keep note of students who did not grasp the technique during the lesson.

Directions for Independent Practice:
1. Ask students to look at their own writing and identify several places where their writing could benefit from additional sensory language. Have students highlight or underline the places where sensory language could be added.
2. Direct students to try out these techniques (10–15 minutes).
3. If students finish early, direct them to begin a new essay/story, read independently, or revise or edit the current piece.

Reteaching ideas:
1. Gather the students who do not grasp the lesson content (as measured through the formative assessment) at a back table while students are writing. Continue guided practice as a group—trying out the different sensory language techniques with the Palacio excerpt.
2. Before students return to their seats, help them identify specific places in their own writing where sensory language could be added. Students should leave this small group with a specific plan for where to add these new details.

Sharing ideas:
1. With a partner, have students read their narratives aloud. Using the Sensory Language Wheel, the listening partners can chart the details that they hear. After reading, the listeners can evaluate how well their partners used sensory language in their narrative.
2. Partners switch roles!

Figure 8.2 Narrative Writing Excerpt for Minilesson

The Cheese Touch
I noticed not too long ago that even though people were getting used to me, no would actually touch me. I didn't realize this at first because it's not like kids go around touching each other that much in middle school, anyways. But last Thursday in dance class, which is, like, my least favorite class, Mrs. Atanabi, the teacher, tried to make Ximena Chin be my dance partner. Now, I've never seen someone have a "panic attack" before, but I have heard about it, and I'm pretty sure Ximena had a panic attack at that second. She got really nervous and turned pale and literally broke into a sweat within a minute, and then she came up with some lame excuse about really having to go to the bathroom. Anyway, Mrs. Atanabi let her off the hook, because she ended up not making anyone dance together.
Then yesterday in my science elective, we were doing this cool mystery-powder investigation where we had to classify a substance as an acid or a base. Everyone had to heat their mystery powders on a heating plate and make observations, so we were all huddled around the powders with our notebooks. Now, there are eight kids in the elective, and several of them were squished together on one side of the plate while one of them—me—had loads of room on the other side. So of course I noticed this, but I was hoping Ms. Rubin wouldn't notice this, because I didn't want her to say something. But of course she did notice this, and of course she said something.
"Guys, there's plenty of room on that side. Tristan, Nino, go over there," she said, so Tristan and Nino scooted over to my side. Tristan and Nino have always been okay-nice to me. I want to go on record as saying that. Not super-nice, like they go out of their way to hang out with me, but okay-nice, like they say hello to me and talk to me like normal. And they didn't even make a face when Ms. Rubin told them to come on my side, which a lot of kids do when they think I'm not looking. Anyway, everything was going fine until Tristan's mystery powder started to melt, too, and I went to move mine off the plate and then my hand accidentally bumped his hand for a fraction of a second. Tristan jerked his hand away so fast he dropped his foil on the floor while knocking everyone else's foil off the heating plate.
"Tristan!" yelled Ms. Rubin, but Tristan didn't even care about the spilled powder on the floor or that he ruined the experiment. What he was most concerned about was getting to the lab sink to wash his hands as fast as possible. That's when I knew for sure that there was a thing about touching me at Beecher Prep.

Source: Palacio (2011, pp. 71–72).

Figure 8.3 Sensory Language Wheel

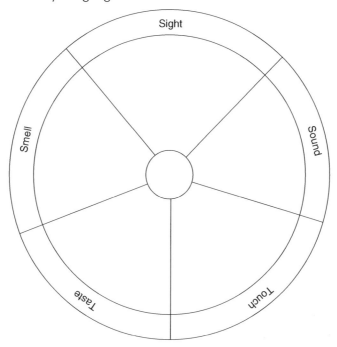

Common Core Connection

The strategies presented in this chapter fit well with the narrative writing standards of the Common Core State Standards (see Table 8.3).

Table 8.3 Narrative Writing Standards

Grade Level	4	5	6
Standard Addressed	**Writing** Write narratives to develop real or imagined experiences or events using effective technique, descriptive details, and clear event sequences.	**Writing** Write narratives to develop real or imagined experiences or events using effective technique, descriptive details, and clear event sequences.	**Writing** Write narratives to develop real or imagined experiences or events using effective technique, relevant descriptive details, and

(*Continued*)

Table 8.3 Continued

Grade Level	4	5	6
	Orient the reader by establishing a situation and introducing a narrator and/or characters; organize an event sequence that unfolds naturally.　Use dialogue and description to develop experiences and events or show the responses of characters to situations.　Use a variety of transitional words and phrases to manage the sequence of events.　Use concrete words and phrases and sensory details to convey experiences and events precisely.　Provide a conclusion that follows from the narrated experiences or events.	Orient the reader by establishing a situation and introducing a narrator and/or characters; organize an event sequence that unfolds naturally.　Use narrative techniques, such as dialogue, description, and pacing, to develop experiences and events or show the responses of characters to situations.　Use a variety of transitional words, phrases, and clauses to manage the sequence of events.　Use concrete words and phrases and sensory details to convey experiences and events precisely.　Provide a conclusion that follows from experiences and events.	well-structured event sequences.　Engage and orient the reader by establishing a context and introducing a narrator and/or characters; organize an event sequence that unfolds naturally and logically.　Use narrative techniques, such as dialogue, pacing, and description, to develop experiences, events, and/or characters.　Use a variety of transition words, phrases, and clauses to convey sequence and signal shifts from one time frame or setting to another.　Use precise words and phrases, relevant descriptive details, and sensory language to convey experiences and events.

Grade Level	4	5	6
			Provide a conclusion that follows from the narrated experiences or events.
	7	**8**	**9–10**
	Writing Write narratives to develop real or imagined experiences or events using effective technique, relevant descriptive details, and well-structured event sequences. a. Engage and orient the reader by establishing a context and point of view and introducing a narrator and/or characters; organize an event sequence that unfolds naturally and logically. b. Use narrative techniques, such as dialogue, pacing, and	**Writing** Write narratives to develop real or imagined experiences or events using effective technique, relevant descriptive details, and well-structured event sequences. a. Engage and orient the reader by establishing a context and point of view and introducing a narrator and/or characters; organize an event sequence that unfolds naturally and logically. b. Use narrative techniques, such as dialogue, pacing, description, and	**Writing** Write narratives to develop real or imagined experiences or events using effective technique, well-chosen details, and well-structured event sequences. Engage and orient the reader by setting out a problem, situation, or observation, establishing one or multiple point(s) of view, and introducing a narrator and/or characters; create a smooth progression of experiences or events. Use narrative techniques, such as dialogue, pacing,

(Continued)

Table 8.3 Continued

	7	8	9–10
	description, to develop experiences, events, and/or characters. c. Use a variety of transition words, phrases, and clauses to convey sequence and signal shifts from one time frame or setting to another. d. Use precise words and phrases, relevant descriptive details, and sensory language to capture the action and convey experiences and events. e. Provide a conclusion that follows from and reflects on the narrated experiences or events.	reflection, to develop experiences, events, and/or characters. c. Use a variety of transition words, phrases, and clauses to convey sequence, signal shifts from one time frame or setting to another, and show the relationships among experiences and events. d. Use precise words and phrases, relevant descriptive details, and sensory language to capture the action and convey experiences and events. e. Provide a conclusion that follows from and reflects on the narrated experiences or events.	description, reflection, and multiple plot lines, to develop experiences, events, and/or characters. Use a variety of techniques to sequence events so that they build on one another to create a coherent whole. Use precise words and phrases, telling details, and sensory language to convey a vivid picture of the experiences, events, setting, and/or characters. Provide a conclusion that follows from and reflects on what is experienced, observed, or resolved over the course of the narrative.

Action Steps

Narrative writing should be an integral part of the language arts experience of all students! It is time to take some action:

1. Which type of personal narrative strategy would fit best with your students, Heart Mapping or Neighborhood Mapping? Why?

_____

_____

2. See if you can match a short story or novel that you already use in your classroom with either prequel, sequel, or alternative–point of view creative writing:

   a. Sequel writing: Title

   _____

   b. Prequel writing: Title

   _____

   c. Alternative point of view: Title

   _____

Works Cited

Atwell, N. (1998). *In the middle: New understandings about writing, reading, and learning.* Portsmouth, NH: Heinemann.

Fletcher, R. (2007). *How to write your life story.* New York: HarperCollins.

Heard, G. (1998). *Awakening the heart: Exploring poetry in elementary and middle school.* Portsmouth, NH: Heinemann.

Howe, J. (2001). *The misfits.* New York: Atheneum.

Howe, J. (2005). *Totally Joe.* New York: Atheneum.

Howe, J. (2011). *Addie on the inside.* New York: Atheneum.

Johnson, E. (2014). Reconceptualizing vulnerability in personal narrative writing with youths. *Journal of Adolescent and Adult Literacy, 57,* 575–583.

Miller, D. (2009). *The book whisperer: Awakening the inner reader in every child.* Indianapolis: Jossey-Bass.

National Governors Association Center for Best Practices & Council of Chief State School Officers. (2010). *Common Core State Standards for English language arts and literacy in history/social studies, science, and technical subjects.* Washington, DC: Authors.

Palacio, R. (2011). *Wonder.* New York: Corgi.

Spinelli, J. (1998). *Knots in my yo-yo string.* New York: Ember.

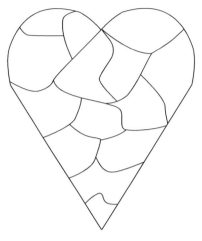

name: _____

Template 8.2 Sensory Language Wheel

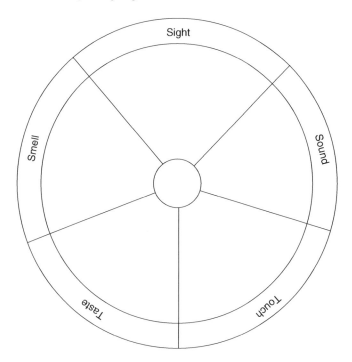

Sight

Sound

Smell

Touch

Taste

Chapter 9

Let Informational Writing Explore a Topic Creatively

I walked into the library to meet the next group of students. They were all on computers, industriously hunting and pecking, swiveling their heads between their keyboards and the screens. I walked over to the teacher to inquire what was happening. "We are doing research," she whispered. "This is our fifth day looking up information for our animal reports." I squinted to see the monitors closest to us. "It looks like this student is on Wikipedia." She shrugged. "Yep, it seems to be where most of them are finding their information."

Why Is This Item on the List So Important?

Informational text writing in most classes is an end product of Googling and searching Wikipedia on a topic, endless graphic organizers with main ideas and supporting details, and haphazard copy and pasting of facts into a word document. What do students learn from this exercise? They learn how to do shoddy research and how to pray that the teacher doesn't catch their plagiarism (if they even recognize that they plagiarized!).

These shadows of research reports are not doing justice to a very important genre of reading and writing. Nonfiction reading has gotten a lot of attention since the Common Core was introduced (I even wrote a whole book about it!), but writing informational texts has often been limited to the foregoing scenario in many classrooms. So many possibilities exist for informational writing (Donovan & Smolkin, 2011)! It is time to recognize these possibilities and break out of the Google/Wikipedia research report box.

Do this—not that principle #9: DO let informational writing explore a topic creatively. DON'T limit informational writing to shallow exploration of a topic.

To Get Started

As addressed in chapter 3, for students to be excellent writers of a genre, they must read excellent examples of that genre. Nonfiction reading can be a trade book, like *Chew on This* (Wilson & Schlosser, 2007). It can be an article from a periodical such as *Time for Kids* or *Scholastic News.* It can be the examination of information in forms such as brochures and pamphlets. But rather than have students simply summarize the information from this reading, we need students to pay close attention to the choices that nonfiction authors make in their writing:

- ♦ *Text structure.* Nonfiction text authors make sophisticated choices when setting up their writing. As students read, direct them to think about the structure of the text (cause and effect, definition, compare and contrast, problem/solution) and why they think the author used it to share the topic (Wilfong, 2014).

- ♦ *Text features.* We often tell students to use the text features of a nonfiction text to help them comprehend, but asking students to pay attention to the why behind them helps to point out author craft: Why would the author use this heading? Why was this pull quote used? Answering these questions helps to prepare students to write their own informational texts that include purposeful text features (Morgan, 2010).

- ♦ *Word choice.* The vocabulary of an informational text is a true reflection of the expertise of the author; if I write a text on cars, there are certain words you would expect me to know and use well. And in order to be able use these words well, I will have to know my topic. It teaches students how to think (and therefore write!) in the academic domain (Whitehead & Murphy, 2014).

Informational Writing Territories. When I begin an informational unit in my classroom, I will often do an exercise like Heart Mapping from chapter 8 to get ideas flowing. Separating out things that are important to us (like in Heart Mapping) versus things we have very strong opinions about (like in

Figure 9.1 Informational Writing Territory

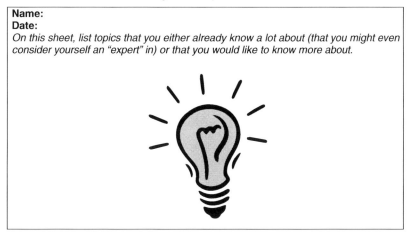

Name:
Date:
On this sheet, list topics that you either already know a lot about (that you might even consider yourself an "expert" in) or that you would like to know more about.

argument writing) is difficult. I will often distribute a page like the one in Figure 9.1 so that students can list things they either already know a lot about or are curious to know more about (a full-size template is included at the end of the chapter). I ask them to consider this list when choosing their informational writing topics but remind them that I would like them to remain objective as they research and write (a difficult task!).

Informational reading is the kind of reading we do the most as college students and adults (Wilfong, 2014). And the same holds true for informational writing: Think back to your college career. How many narratives did you get to write? I am guessing you got to write a few here or there. Now think about the all-nighters you pulled writing papers—those were summaries of readings, syntheses of research, and proposals of new ideas. Examine the kinds of writing you do as an adult—when was the last time you wrote fiction? The types of writing we do now center on e-mails, memos, briefs, and synthesizing ideas to present to others. This is the kind of writing we must prepare students to do.

Instructional Practices to Update

Updated Strategy #1: Break Up With the Five-Paragraph Essay in Favor of More Creative Ways to Write Informational Text

The five-paragraph essay has endured as a format for informational writing because it works. It is a formula that pretty much any information can be plugged into: an introduction that starts as off as general and ends in a thesis statement, and three body paragraphs with an introductory statement, three supporting details, and a concluding statement. It ends with a conclusion that restates the introduction. As teachers, we have to recognize that this is one type of writing, but *it is not the only type of writing* (Campbell, 2014). If you are saying to yourself right now, "Well, I make my students have eight details, not three," do not pat yourself on the back. You are still carrying on the cause of the five-paragraph essay.

Nowhere in the writing literature does it say that a good piece of informational (or any other genre of writing) must be five paragraphs. In fact, recently, researchers have stated that the five-paragraph essay reflects a deficit teaching model—that we don't trust our students to produce beyond formula writing (Brannon et al., 2008). Nowhere does it say that you need a certain number of details to really support your thesis statement. This has been an unspoken rule that we teachers have adopted as law for far too long.

It is time to break up with the five-paragraph essay. I offer a breakup note in Figure 9.2.

(Pause to wipe away tears.)

Figure 9.2 Breaking Up With the Five-Paragraph Essay

Dear Five-Paragraph Essay,

I pen this letter to let you know that it is time to move on. Although you have offered my students and me comfort with your predictable ways, I find that your formula is starting to stifle the creativity and needs of my students. I will still revisit you yearly to remind students that you are a form that is available to them, but I will no longer teach you and only you. Please let the hamburger paragraph graphic organizer know the news.

Sincerely,

Mrs. Red Pen

Figure 9.3 presents a list of the many, many forms of nonfiction writing that students could use to share information. This list is long. If you presented

Figure 9.3 Forms of Informational Text Writing

Autobiography	Biography	Brochures
Encyclopedia or Wiki entries	Essays How-to articles	Interviews
Letters Magazine articles	News articles	Pamphlets	Picture book
PowerPoint presentation/Prezi	Report	Research brief	Speeches	Summary

Source: Adapted from Williams (2014).

this entire list to students, you would get an amazing continuum of work from students struggling to fit into this genre.

I prefer to narrow informational text formats down, depending on the purpose of the writing. This allows me to select and teach text structure appropriate to these formats. I am better able to scaffold student informational writing experiences without stifling their creativity. This is referred to as bounded choice (Gambrell, 2011). You are still allowing students to choose a format that appeals to them, but not offering too many choices that will result in limited instruction. Table 9.1 presents the forms of informational writing by purpose. This table also helps me narrow down the kinds of nonfiction reading my students should do to suit our writing purposes.

To inform, describe, and explain are very close cousins on the informational writing spectrum. I separate the three in my mind by considering a topic, such as spiders. Informing someone about a spider would be brief—I would present the most important facts in a concise format. Describing a spider would look like your basic report: what it is, what it looks like, what it eats, life cycle, and so forth. You can't *explain* a spider; you describe it! Explanations examine an action: I might examine how a spider spins a web, for example. Clarifying your purposes for teaching informational writing (to inform, to describe, or to explain) will help clarify your students' writing.

Table 9.1 Forms of Informational Writing by Purpose

To inform	To describe	To explain
•Wiki/Encyclopedia Entry	•Essay	How-to text
•Interview	•Report	•Essay
•Summarize	•Speech	•Report
•Research brief	•Letter	•Speech
	•Brochure	•Letter
	•News article	•Pamphlet
	•PowerPoint/Prezi	•Magazine article
	•Magazine article	•PowerPoint/Prezi
	•Picture book	
	•Autobiography	
	•Biography	

Updated Strategy #2: Teach Kids to Be Savvy Consumers of Informational Text in Order to Write About a Topic Effectively

Let's return to the anecdote at the beginning of the chapter and continue the research journey those students were on. It began with the Googling and Wikipedia-ing, and then continued to the note carding. "Note carding" is another made-up verb that describes the process that teachers instruct students to use when gathering facts on a topic. A fact is written on each card, later to be sorted into categories for the next step, outlining (not a made-up verb this time). An outline is created from these note cards, grouping facts together into paragraphs to inform, to describe, and/or to explain. The intent is good: to teach students how to gather information from a variety of sources in order to write about a topic. The process is tedious. And through it all, something is missing: the ability to read a nonfiction text, pull out what is important, and discard the rest. We think we are accomplishing that with the note carding stage, but a flip through the note cards that the students wrote for their reports were sentences copied from Internet sources without reason. This is handwriting practicing!

Students need direct instruction on how to be savvy consumers of nonfiction text in order to be able to write it effectively. Here are the steps to take to make that happen:

1. *Start with the end in mind*. Students often enter the computer lab clueless about what they want to learn about their topic. That is when the mindless searching begins, reading pointless articles to find a piece of information that fits with their ideas. A minilesson on identifying search terms is necessary to make the best use of your time:

    ♦ Begin by having students write two sentences about their topic. From there, they underline key words—an initial set of search terms.

    ♦ Next, students identify synonyms of their key words to use when conducting research.

    ♦ Finally, students think of broader categories in which their key words and synonyms fall. This final list is a backup plan in case their initial search terms do not yield enough results (Samuels, 2004).

    Figure 9.4 contains steps in this process to help guide students, while Figure 9.5 contains an example of this process.

2. Once the search terms are determined, they can be entered into a data collection sheet similar to the one presented in Figure 9.6 (a full-size template is included at the end of the chapter).

3. *Choose a better database*. Let's face it: Google and Wikipedia are just not getting it done. EBSCOHost, a research database carried by most

public libraries, has collections specifically for elementary, middle, and high school students. *Primary Search* is for elementary-aged students, *Middle Search Plus* is for middle school students, and *MAS Ultra* is for high school students. There are others out there, but these are my go-tos for helping students find age-appropriate research.

4. *Reading for research.* True confession time: When I research something (like this book), I do not read every word of every article and book that I pull. Neither should your students! The point of being a good researcher is being able to find what you want in an expedient manner. I demonstrated this to a group of eighth graders this semester:

We were in a computer lab, using the Middle Search Plus database. Students were using their search lenses to find articles on topics they were researching for their American History classes, saving them to a folder on the server, and then settling in to read. I noticed that Jameer had his head down. "What's going on, Jameer?" He gestured to his computer. "I found fifteen articles about Ben Franklin's role in the American Revolution." "That's great!" I replied. "And the problem is?" "I now have to read fifteen articles about Ben Franklin's role in the American Revolution!" he complained. I stopped the class. "Are you all finding better articles now that you have narrowed down your search terms?" Heads nodded in my direction. "Now I want to show you a secret to conducting research when writing something informational." I called Jameer up to the demonstration computer. "Jameer is going to pull up his article folder for us and open up his first article." The colorful PDF opened on the front screen. "See this box right here?" I asked, pointing to the search box in the PDF viewer. Heads nodded again. "I use this when I am reading research to help me search within a document for quotes and facts to use to support myself." I looked at Jameer. "What is one thing that you want to support in your paper?" He looked at his graphic organizer. "I want to know how important he was to the American Revolution." I typed in "Benjamin Franklin important" into the search box of the PDF. Thumbnails populated the left side of the screen. "See right here?" I asked students. "This will tell me where in the document I should begin looking to really get at the information I want." Stunned faces looked back at me. "Isn't that cheating?" Shyla asked. "You will still be doing plenty of reading," I replied. "And you may end up reading the whole article, anyways. But it is a way to help you get started." I looked at Jameer, who was already writing down the first fact in his graphic organizer. "Better?" I asked him. I got a thumbs-up in return.

5. *From bullet points to paragraphs.* At this point, students should have information to turn into true paragraphs. This is when rules (e.g., you need three supporting details for each thesis statement) and graphic organizers are often brought out. Another graphic organizer here is overkill—you are literally using a graphic organizer for your graphic organizer! What is needed is more modeling—a perfect minilesson opportunity to show students how to take a list of facts and quotes and turn them into an artful paragraph. Guided practice could be students working together or in small groups to try their hand at the same idea. And then independent practice is them working on their own list of facts and quotes and turning them into paragraphs. Aren't you tired of reading the same essay over and over again? Confining graphic organizers can do that to writing. Let students try something new!

Figure 9.4   Creating Effective Search Terms

1.   Write one or two sentences about your topic.
2.   Underline key words in the sentences you wrote in step 1.
3.   Place these key words into a list.
4.   Add synonyms of these key words to that list.
5.   Consider adding words of broader categories that your key words fall into.
6.   Consider adding any subtopic words to your list.

Source: Adapted from Samuels (2004).

Figure 9.5   Sample Search Term Process

1.   Write one or two sentences about your topic. **What is the history of school uniforms? Do they really help students pay attention better in class?**
2.   Underline key words in the sentences you wrote in step 1. **What is the *history of school uniforms*? Do they really *help students pay attention better in class*?**
3.   Place these key words into a list. **School uniforms** **History of school uniforms** **Help students pay attention in class**
4.   Add synonyms of these key words to that list. **School uniforms, *coordinated outfits, regiment, common attire***

History of school uniforms, *record, account* **Help students pay attention in class,** *behavior, distractions*
5.   Consider adding words of broader categories that your key words fall into. **School uniforms,** *coordinated outfits, regiment, common attire* **History of school uniforms,** *record, account* **Help students pay attention in class,** *behavior, distractions* *Use in private schools, public schools*
6.   Consider adding any subtopic words to your list. **School uniforms,** *coordinated outfits, regiment, common attire* **History of school uniforms,** *record, account* **Help students pay attention in class,** *behavior, distractions, why use them* *Use in private schools, public schools*

Figure 9.6   Data Collection Sheet

Topic

#1:

#2

#3

#4

#5

Content Area Connection

A Captain Obvious statement: Content area teachers, this entire chapter applies to you! Informative writing is included in the Literacy Standards for History, Science, and Other Technical Subjects, grades 6–12. Informative writing in the content areas can often be limited to lab reports in science and document-based questions in history. Content area teachers need to consider a few points as they broaden the purposes and formats for writing in their classrooms:

◆ *Word choice is paramount in the content areas.* In order to be an expert of a domain, students must attend to the vocabulary necessary to demonstrate mastery of content (Kohen, 2013). If students are to write about a content area topic, it can be helpful to have them create their own academic glossary of terms that they should include in their writing.

◆ *Pay attention to domain-specific structures.* What kinds of structures and formats do scientists, historians, and mathematicians use? Using these structures and formats with purpose in the content area classrooms encourages students to think like the scholars of those domains (Montelongo & Herter, 2010; Morgan, 2010).

◆ *Think about ways to use writing in your classroom without revision.* Writing does not always have to be a formal process in the content area classroom. How can you encourage students to write about the content to demonstrate knowledge, warm up their brains, and dig deeper into ideas? Consider entrance and exit slips, Think-Pair-Share, alphabet books, and more to make writing an everyday activity in your classroom (Wilcox & Munroe, 2011).

Sample minilesson: "Writing excellent informational writing introductions."

As promised, here is a minilesson to use in conjunction with informational writing, although it can be just as appropriate for narrative and argument writing, too!

Table 9.2 Informational Writing Minilesson

Unit/Genre: Informational Writing
Complete standard: *Introduce a topic clearly, previewing what is to follow; organize ideas, concepts, and information, using strategies such as definition, classification, comparison/contrast, and cause/effect; include formatting (e.g., headings), graphics (e.g., charts, tables), and multimedia when useful to aiding comprehension.* **Portion of the standard for emphasis in this lesson:** *Introduce a topic clearly, previewing what is to follow.*

Modeling:

1. Display sample text for students to read (see Figure 9.7).
2. Read text aloud to students.
3. Introduce teaching point on anchor chart. Ask students to turn to an elbow buddy or small group and discuss: What is the purpose of an introduction in writing informational text (30 seconds for discussion)?
4. Solicit answers from students; select best definition and add it to anchor chart.
5. Distribute handout titled "Techniques That Will Hook Your Readers" (Figure 9.8). Introduce techniques two at a time. Ask students to show their favorite by holding up the number of fingers that corresponds to the number of the technique they like best.
6. After introducing all five techniques, ask students to choose one for you to model with the writing sample.
7. Using their request, write a new introduction for the sample, thinking aloud your writing process and writing in front of students.

Guided Practice:

1. In small groups, have students choose one or two different introductory techniques from the handout and collaboratively try out the techniques on the writing sample (5–7 minutes, depending on proficiency of students).
2. Formative assessment: Have small groups share their new introductions. Students share the technique that they tried and then read their introductions for the group. Keep note of students who did not grasp the technique during the lesson.

Directions for Independent Practice:

1. Ask students to look at their own writing and identify one or two introductory techniques that they think will mesh well with their informative essays. Have students hold up the number of the technique they plan on trying first.
2. Direct students to try out these techniques (10–15 minutes).
3. If students finish early, direct them to begin a new essay/story, read independently, or revise or edit the current piece.

Reteaching ideas:

1. Gather the students who do not grasp the lesson content (as measured through the formative assessment) at a back table while students are writing. Continue guided practice as a group—trying out the different introduction techniques together with the writing sample.
2. Before students return to their seats, help them identify a technique that will work for their writing.

(*Continued*)

Figure 9.7 Writing Sample for Introduction Minilesson

Prompt: Describe a fabulous meal you have had. What was it? Why was it so delicious?
The best meal that I have ever had was my mom's Chicken Kiev. If you are not familiar with Chicken Kiev, it is a chicken breast, pounded flat, stuffed with butter and parsley, breaded, and fried. When you cut into it, butter oozes out, coating your plate with happiness (and clogging your arteries with cholesterol). You get all of your taste buds satisfied with Chicken Kiev—crunchy, salty, buttery goodness on a plate!

Figure 9.8 Handout—Techniques That Will Hook Your Readers

1. Dialogue
"Hurry or you'll be late!" called my mother from the bottom of the stairs. "Today of all days you want to be on time." If I had only known what that day would bring, I would have stayed in bed.
2. A Question
Have you ever had a day when you wished you had stayed in bed? As I rushed to catch the bus on what seemed to be a perfectly normal day I had no idea what was ahead of me.
3. A Vivid Description
The sun was warm on my back as I raced toward the waiting yellow school bus. As I nestled into the worn leather seat I was greeted by the friendly voices of other excited children. The look on my face was one of confidence and contentment. With a jerk the bus rumbled down the road, and I was on my way into one of the worst days of my life.
4. An Interesting Fact
Shock has been known to kill 10-year-olds. It can cause their brains to explode and their heart to stop dead still. These facts raced through my mind as I stood dumbfounded in front of my fourth-grade classmates. I wish I had stayed in bed!
5. Sound Effects
"Buzzzzzz!" The sound of my alarm clock droned in my ears as I struggled to come awake. With a start I sat straight up in my bed. This was my big day, and I had to be on time.

Common Core Connection

The informational and research writing standards for English/Language Arts and informational writing standard for Literacy Standards for History/Social Studies, Science, and Other Technical Subjects fit well with the strategies discussed in this chapter (see Table 9.3).

Table 9.3 English/Language Arts Standards

Grade Level	4	5	6
Standard Addressed	**Writing** Write informative/ explanatory texts to examine a topic and convey ideas and information clearly. a. Introduce a topic clearly and group related information in paragraphs and sections; include formatting (e.g., headings), illustrations, and multimedia when useful to aiding comprehension. b. Develop the topic with facts, definitions, concrete details, quotations, or other information and examples related to the topic. c. Link ideas within categories of information using words and phrases (e.g., *another, for example, also, because*).	**Writing** Write informative/ explanatory texts to examine a topic and convey ideas and information clearly. Introduce a topic clearly, provide a general observation and focus, and group related information logically; include formatting (e.g., headings), illustrations, and multimedia when useful to aiding comprehension. Develop the topic with facts, definitions, concrete details, quotations, or other information and examples related to the topic. Link ideas within and across categories of information using words,	**Writing** Write informative/ explanatory texts to examine a topic and convey ideas, concepts, and information through the selection, organization, and analysis of relevant content. Introduce a topic; organize ideas, concepts, and information, using strategies such as definition, classification, comparison/ contrast, and cause/ effect; include formatting (e.g., headings), graphics (e.g., charts, tables), and multimedia when useful to aiding comprehension. Develop the topic with relevant facts, definitions, concrete details, quotations,

(Continued)

Table 9.3 Continued

Grade Level	4	5	6
	d. Use precise language and domain-specific vocabulary to inform about or explain the topic. e. Provide a concluding statement or section related to the information or explanation presented. Conduct short research projects that build knowledge through investigation of different aspects of a topic. Recall relevant information from experiences or gather relevant information from print and digital sources; take notes and categorize information, and provide a list of sources.	phrases, and clauses (e.g., *in contrast, especially*). Use precise language and domain-specific vocabulary to inform about or explain the topic. Provide a concluding statement or section related to the information or explanation presented. Conduct short research projects that use several sources to build knowledge through investigation of different aspects of a topic. Recall relevant information from experiences or gather relevant information from print and digital sources; summarize or paraphrase information in notes and finished work, and provide a list of sources.	or other information and examples. Use appropriate transitions to clarify the relationships among ideas and concepts. Use precise language and domain-specific vocabulary to inform about or explain the topic. Establish and maintain a formal style. Provide a concluding statement or section that follows from the information or explanation presented. Conduct short research projects to answer a question, drawing on several sources and refocusing the inquiry when appropriate. Gather relevant information from multiple

Grade Level	4	5	6
			print and digital sources; assess the credibility of each source; and quote or paraphrase the data and conclusions of others while avoiding plagiarism and providing basic bibliographic information for sources.
	7	**8**	**9–10**
	Writing Write informative/ explanatory texts to examine a topic and convey ideas, concepts, and information through the selection, organization, and analysis of relevant content. Introduce a topic clearly, previewing what is to follow; organize ideas, concepts, and information, using strategies such as definition,	**Writing** Write informative/ explanatory texts to examine a topic and convey ideas, concepts, and information through the selection, organization, and analysis of relevant content. Introduce a topic clearly, previewing what is to follow; organize ideas, concepts, and information into broader categories; include	**Writing** Write informative/ explanatory texts to examine and convey complex ideas, concepts, and information clearly and accurately through the effective selection, organization, and analysis of content. Introduce a topic; organize complex ideas, concepts, and information to make important connections and

(Continued)

Table 9.3 Continued

	7	8	9–10
	classification, comparison/ contrast, and cause/ effect; include formatting (e.g., headings), graphics (e.g., charts, tables), and multimedia when useful to aiding comprehension. Develop the topic with relevant facts, definitions, concrete details, quotations, or other information and examples. Use appropriate transitions to create cohesion and clarify the relationships among ideas and concepts. Use precise language and domain-specific vocabulary to inform about or explain the topic. Establish and maintain a formal style.	formatting (e.g., headings), graphics (e.g., charts, tables), and multimedia when useful to aiding comprehension. Develop the topic with relevant, well-chosen facts, definitions, concrete details, quotations, or other information and examples. Use appropriate and varied transitions to create cohesion and clarify the relationships among ideas and concepts. Use precise language and domain-specific vocabulary to inform about or explain the topic. Establish and maintain a formal style. Provide a concluding statement or	distinctions; include formatting (e.g., headings), graphics (e.g., figures, tables), and multimedia when useful to aiding comprehension. Develop the topic with well-chosen, relevant, and sufficient facts, extended definitions, concrete details, quotations, or other information and examples appropriate to the audience's knowledge of the topic. Use appropriate and varied transitions to link the major sections of the text, create cohesion, and clarify the relationships among complex ideas and concepts.

	7	8	9–10
	Provide a concluding statement or section that follows from and supports the information or explanation presented. Conduct short research projects to answer a question, drawing on several sources and generating additional related, focused questions for further research and investigation. Gather relevant information from multiple print and digital sources, using search terms effectively; assess the credibility and accuracy of each source; and quote or paraphrase the data and conclusions of others while avoiding	section that follows from and supports the information or explanation presented. Conduct short research projects to answer a question (including a self-generated question), drawing on several sources and generating additional related, focused questions that allow for multiple avenues of exploration. Gather relevant information from multiple print and digital sources, using search terms effectively; assess the credibility and accuracy of each source; and quote or paraphrase the data and conclusions of others while avoiding	Use precise language and domain-specific vocabulary to manage the complexity of the topic. Establish and maintain a formal style and objective tone while attending to the norms and conventions of the discipline in which they are writing. Provide a concluding statement or section that follows from and supports the information or explanation presented (e.g., articulating implications or the significance of the topic). Conduct short as well as more sustained research projects to answer a question (including a self-generated question) or

(Continued)

Table 9.3 Continued

	7	8	9–10
	plagiarism and following a standard format for citation.	plagiarism and following a standard format for citation.	solve a problem; narrow or broaden the inquiry when appropriate; synthesize multiple sources on the subject, demonstrating understanding of the subject under investigation. Gather relevant information from multiple authoritative print and digital sources, using advanced searches effectively; assess the usefulness of each source in answering the research question; integrate information into the text selectively to maintain the flow of ideas, avoiding plagiarism and following a standard format for citation.

Literacy Standards for History/Social Studies, Science, and Other Technical Subjects

	6–8	9–10

	Writing
	Write informative/ explanatory texts, including the narration of historical events, scientific procedures/ experiments, or technical processes.
	
	    Introduce a topic clearly, previewing what is to follow; organize ideas, concepts, and information into broader categories as appropriate to achieving purpose; include formatting (e.g., headings), graphics (e.g., charts, tables), and multimedia when useful to aiding comprehension.
	    Develop the topic with relevant, well-chosen facts, definitions, concrete details, quotations, or other information and examples.
	    Use appropriate and varied transitions to create cohesion and clarify the relationships among ideas and concepts.
	    Use precise language and domain-specific
		Writing
		Write informative/ explanatory texts, including the narration of historical events, scientific procedures/ experiments, or technical processes.
		
		    Introduce a topic and organize ideas, concepts, and information to make important connections and distinctions; include formatting (e.g., headings), graphics (e.g., figures, tables), and multimedia when useful to aiding comprehension.
		    Develop the topic with well-chosen, relevant, and sufficient facts, extended definitions, concrete details, quotations, or other information and examples appropriate to the audience's knowledge of the topic.
		    Use varied transitions and sentence structures to link the major sections of the text, create cohesion, and clarify the relationships among ideas and concepts.

	6–8	9–10
	vocabulary to inform about or explain the topic. Establish and maintain a formal style and objective tone. Provide a concluding statement or section that follows from and supports the information or explanation presented.	Use precise language and domain-specific vocabulary to manage the complexity of the topic and convey a style appropriate to the discipline and context as well as to the expertise of likely readers. Establish and maintain a formal style and objective tone while attending to the norms and conventions of the discipline in which they are writing. Provide a concluding statement or section that follows from and supports the information or explanation presented (e.g., articulating implications or the significance of the topic).

Action Steps

Informational writing may actually end up being the favorite type of writing for you and your students with a few changes! It is time to take some action . . .

1. What kind of informational reading are you using in your classroom? What techniques can you identify to point out to your students when reading these mentor texts?

   a. Title:_____

      Technique and page number: _____

   b. Title:_____

      Technique and page number: _____

   c. Title:_____

      Technique and page number: _____

2. What genres could you see yourself offering as choices to your students beyond the five-paragraph essay? List them here:

   _____

   _____

   _____

   _____

3. Do a little prep work to teach the research lesson described in Strategy #2:

   a. Write one or two sentences about your topic.

      _____

      _____

   b. Underline key words in the sentences you wrote in step 1.

   c. Place these key words into a list.

      _____

      _____

   d. Add synonyms of these key words to that list.

      _____

      _____

e. Consider adding words of broader categories that your key words fall into.

_____

_____

f. Consider adding any subtopic words to your list.

_____

_____

Works Cited

Brannon, L., Courtney, J., Urbanski, C., Woodward, S., Reynolds, J., Iannone, A., . . . Haag, K. (2008). The five-paragraph essay and the deficit model of education. *English Journal, 98*, 16–21.

Campbell, K. (2014). Beyond the five-paragraph essay. *Educational Leadership, 71*, 60–65.

Donovan, C., & Smolkin, L. (2011). Supporting informational writing in the elementary grades. *Reading Teacher, 64*, 406–416.

Gambrell, L. (2011). Seven rules of engagement: What's most important to know about motivation to read. *Reading Teacher, 65*, 172–178.

Kohen, A. (2013). Informational writing in high school science: The importance of genre, apprenticeship, and publication. *Journal of Adolescent and Adult Literacy, 57*, 233–242.

Montelongo, J., & Herter, R. (2010). Using technology to support expository reading and writing in science class. *Science Activities, 47*, 89–102.

Morgan, D. (2010). Writing feature articles with intermediate students. *Reading Teacher, 64*, 181–189.

Samuels, H. (2004). Listing key words. Retrieved from www.crlsresearchguide.org/02_Listing_Key_Words.asp

Whitehead, D., & Murphy, F. (2014). "Mind your language": High school students write laboratory reports. *Journal of Adolescent and Adult Literacy, 57*, 492–502.

Wilcox, B., & Munroe, E. (2011). Integrating writing and mathematics. *Reading Teacher, 64*, 521–529.

Wilfong, L. (2014). *Nonfiction reading that works: Do this—not that!* New York: Routledge.

Williams, S. (2014). Forms of writing. Retrieved from www.suzanne-williams.com/formsof.htm

Wilson, C., & Schlosser. E. (2007). *Chew on this: Everything you don't want to know about fast food.* Boston: Houghton Mifflin.

Template 9.1   Informational Writing Territory

Name:
Date:
On this sheet, list topics that you either already know a lot about (that you might even consider yourself an "expert" in) or that you would like to know more about.

Template 9.2   Data Collection Sheet

Topic

#1:
-
-
-

#2
-
-
-

#3
-
-
-

#4
-
-
-

#5
-
-
-

© 2015, *Writing Strategies That Work,* Lori G. Wilfong, Routledge

Template 9.3   Techniques That Will Hook Your Readers

1. Dialogue
"Hurry or you'll be late!" called my mother from the bottom of the stairs. "Today of all days you want to be on time." If I had only known what that day would bring, I would have stayed in bed.
2. A Question
Have you ever had a day when you wished you had stayed in bed? As I rushed to catch the bus on what seemed to be a perfectly normal day, I had no idea what was ahead of me.
3. A Vivid Description
The sun was warm on my back as I raced toward the waiting yellow school bus. As I nestled into the worn leather seat, I was greeted by the friendly voices of other excited children. The look on my face was one of confidence and contentment. With a jerk the bus rumbled down the road, and I was on my way into one of the worst days of my life.
4. An Interesting Fact
Shock has been known to kill 10-year-olds. It can cause their brains to explode and their heart to stop dead still. These facts raced through my mind as I stood dumbfounded in front of my fourth fourth-grade classmates. I wish I had stayed in bed!
5. Sound Effects
"Buzzzzzz!" The sound of my alarm clock droned in my ears as I struggled to come awake. With a start I sat straight up in my bed. This was my big day, and I had to be on time.

Chapter 10

Let Argument Writing Be Situated in Real-World Application

My students wanted an extension on a deadline for a multigenre project they were writing. "Convince me," I wrote back to the group e-mail. "Justify your position and I will consider it." Never in my dreams did I think that when I arrived in my classroom two days later that I would be greeted with a PowerPoint presentation, complete with facts to support a due date extension, as well as a white paper that probably took up valuable multigenre paper time, full of well-crafted arguments. "You did it," I said to the students. "How can I ignore your request when you present your side so convincingly?"

Why Is This Item on the List So Important?

Is there anything more natural to the preteen or teenager than arguing? Later bedtimes, less homework, more device time—our students are primed and ready to give opinions and arguments at the drop of a hat! Argument and evidence were named as the two "anchor" standards of the Common Core State Standards; our students have argument down, but often lack the evidence to back themselves up.

Argument writing and informational writing share the characteristics of nonfiction text: They are both situated in real-world principles and teach about a topic. Writing in either genre can take many forms beyond the five-paragraph essay. Argument, however, does more than just inform, describe, or explain (although it may need these elements to be effective): A good argument will persuade, advise, analyze, review, or comment (Andrews et al., 2009).

To teach students how to craft exceptional arguments, we need to capitalize on their natural proclivity to argue for something they want and apply those same principles to argument writing across content areas. Encouraging these skills prepares students for the kind of writing necessary for success later in their lives (Moore & MacArthur, 2011). As George Hillocks states, "Argument is at the heart of critical thinking and academic discourse" (Hillocks, 2011, p. xvii).

> **Do this—not that principle #10:** *DO let argument writing be situated in real-world application. DON'T limit argument writing to one-sided, "what-if" debates.*

To Get Started

Think of the "before" picture of argument writing, or persuasion as you most likely called it in your classroom. You taught them the three types of appeals: pathos, logos, and ethos. You studied glittering generalities in commercials and propaganda in World War II posters, and reviewed political cartoons as an alternative form of persuasion. At the end of the day (or unit), students had a sense that companies were trying to pull a fast one on them, and they had a basic understanding of persuasive writing.

The shift necessary to teach argument (grades 6–12) or opinion (grades K–5) was once described to me like this: Argument is persuasion minus the passion. I actually prefer to think of argument as being full of passion, but it includes the credibility to make the writer's stance viable, through evidence and reasons.

Argument writing has the capacity to become every student's favorite time in class. By allowing students to choose topics that matter, by infusing our classrooms with important arguments that impact our world, most students can't help but be swept up in the excitement of learning and writing about something that counts (Chapman, Hobbel, & Alvarado, 2011).

RAFTS to float argumentative writing. I find that helping students situate their writing using a RAFT is helpful in developing context (Dean, 2006; Santa, Havens, & Valdes, 2004; Wilfong, 2014). Students use this graphic

Table 10.1 RAFT Template

Role	Audience	Format	Topic

organizer to lay out their role as the Writer (R), the audience for whom the writing is intended (A), the format that the writing will take (F), and the topic that will be addressed (T). Table 10.1 is a blank RAFT template (a full-sized template is included at the end of the chapter).

By helping students define the context of their paper early in the writing process, we are developing voice and style, keys to good argument writing. If I am writing a paper to convince my parents to allow me to get a puppy, my voice and style would be very different than that of a concerned parent writing the school board to request that the school day be extended.

Format. I promise that I won't rant again regarding the five-paragraph essay. Instead, I will provide a list of formats appropriate for argumentative writing and its purposes in Table 10.2.

Table 10.2 Appropriate Formats for Argumentative Writing

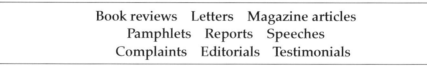

Book reviews   Letters   Magazine articles
Pamphlets   Reports   Speeches
Complaints   Editorials   Testimonials

Instructional Practices to Update

Updated Strategy #1: Use the CREW Strategy to Assist Students in Identifying, Analyzing, and Writing Effective Arguments

The Toulmin model of argument (1958) has been a trusted teaching practice for many years (Warren, 2010). Toulmin clarified the idea of the "claim" in argument—your stance on the topic—and then made his own claim that for an argument to be sound, it must be supported by data. Fast-forward 56 years, and Toulmin's model has been expanded to include the claim, reasons, evidence, and warrant (Warren, 2010).

A colleague, Andrew Pinney, took Toulmin's model of argument and created a reading and writing strategy to assist students in identifying, analyzing, and writing effective arguments. Together, he and I polished the strategy to teach all elements of arguments to students across the content areas and named it the CREW strategy. Here are the steps to use the CREW strategy in your own classroom:

1. Introduce the parts of an effective argument to students (provided in Table 10.3). Model different examples of each element for students.

2. Provide an argumentative text for students to read. One of my favorite resources for a wide variety of argumentative texts is the "Room for Debate" site on the *New York Times* website. They examine a single topic, such as celebrity plastic surgery, and present a variety of opinions on that topic by experts. A new topic is explored every day.

3. Model annotating the text using the CREW strategy—think aloud, reading each sentence and trying to figure out how each sentence fits into the CREW designations.

4. Present a new text to students. Have them use the CREW strategy to annotate the text. After reading, direct students to meet with a partner or small group to compare annotations. There is no answer key for this activity; you are listening to see if students can give a rationale for their annotations.

5. Distribute the CREW collector sheet to students (Figure 10.1). Model how to take your annotations and collect them in each category to dissect the author's argument. Give students time to collect their own argument elements from the first text.

Table 10.3   Parts of an Effective Argument

C	**CLAIM**—A debatable and defensible statement	LeBron James is the best basketball player in the NBA.
R	**REASON**—General support for a claim	LeBron is a high scorer.
E	**EVIDENCE**—Specific support for Claim and Reason	As of February 2013, LeBron was averaging 27.3 points per game, and he scored more than 30 points in seven consecutive games, at the age of 28.
W	**WARRANT**—Conclusion that brings it all together	A high-scoring basketball player is a good basketball player.

Figure 10.1   CREW Collector Sheet

Text 1 Title:	Text 2 Title:
Claim:	Claim:
Reason: 1. _____ 2. _____ 3. _____	Reason: 1. _____ 2. _____ 3. _____
Evidence: 1. _____ 2. _____ 3. _____	Evidence: 1. _____ 2. _____ 3. _____
Warrant:	Warrant:

6. Distribute a second argumentative text on a similar topic to students. Go through steps 4 and 5 with this second text.

After reading both texts, a few follow-up actions can take place:

- ♦ Students can analyze the strength of each author's argument, using their CREW collector sheet.

- ♦ Students can write an analysis of the topic, using the argument elements they collected.

- ♦ Students can begin to write their own arguments, using these texts as mentor texts!

The strengths of this strategy lie in its applicability to any argumentative text. Across content areas, argument texts can be analyzed and compared using the CREW strategy.

Updated Strategy #2: Using the Book Battle to Bring Argument and Debate to the ELA Class

Argument in the language arts class can lack the pizazz that argument can take on in the content areas. It is one thing to structure an argument about global warming or conflicts around the world; it is another to structure an argument about theme, plot, or characterization. To combat the low-level energy that argument writing about literature can possess, I created a Book Battle for students to take part in, March Madness style.

A Book Battle taps into student interest and motivation by allowing them to choose a book to "battle" on, crafting short arguments to best an opponent. Figure 10.2 presents a Book Battle Bracket (a full-sized template is included at the end of the chapter).

I usually hold a Book Battle at the midpoint and end of the year. I invite students to bring in the best book they have read so far during this academic year. The genre does not matter; it just has to be a book that they are passionate enough about to put up against other books. As a class, we set up our bracket; I pair up students who chose the same book to work together (there are always a few) and then list students as competitors in the bracket.

Students are then given 3 minutes to craft an argument as to why this book is the best book. Note cards are provided so that students can list talking points for the debate. They are allowed to use resources to construct their arguments, but I remind them to not use all of their best evidence at in the beginning—they never know if their book will move on in the bracket!

I call the first two students up to the front of the room. They are given 2 minutes to present their arguments each. I then pull in a little technology: Using www.polleverywhere.com, I have students vote via text or computer on which book should move on in the Book Battle. Figure 10.3 shows a sample text poll. I find that students are thrilled to be allowed to use their cell phones in the classroom, and it keeps voting anonymous.

After we go through the round of 16, students work to create their next argument for the next round of debate. Students whose books didn't move on pair up with a winner to help write the next set of arguments (ensuring that participation remains high).

The arguments that students wrote for this strategy were incredible! They pulled in author facts and tidbits from the book, and used literary elements like theme and plot to make their points. It made argument writing relevant and fun for students.

Figure 10.2   Book Battle Template

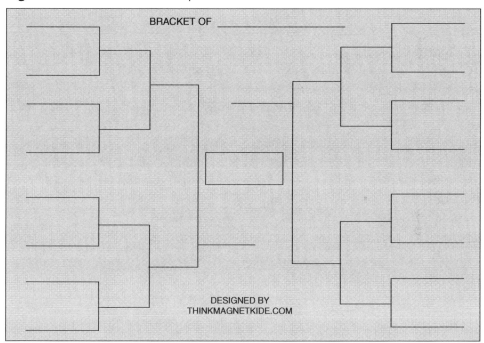

Figure 10.3   Sample Text Poll

Which book should move on in the Book Battle?	
The Adoration of Jenna Fox	**486078**
Dash and Lily's Book of Dares	**486089**

A few adaptions exist for this strategy across content areas: A social studies colleague used this in his classroom to help students learn content from 20th-century U.S. history. He gave students a list of the most important events and people from the 20th century and had students spend a day researching facts on their topic. He then set them in a battle bracket. Students debated the importance of their topic over that of their opponents, leading up to a supreme event or person from the 20th century. Each round, students had to find new facts and ideas to support their arguments. In a science classroom, I have watched students debate the importance of different elements and the merits of a variety of scientists using the Book Battle technique. Each time, content and argument strategies were evident in students' impassioned presentations—so much better than the usual oral reports given in classes!

Content Area Connection

Argument writing is clearly defined for social studies and science teachers in the Common Core State Standards. Just as with informative writing, students need to think about the arguments that are appropriate for specific content areas. Scientists, for example, must be able to argue about why an experiment is significant and adds to the existing literature for a topic (Sampson et al., 2013). Historians debate the actions that important historical figures take and the impact these actions have on us today. The key to making argument a vital part of a content area class is making sure it is more than just an "extra": something that you are doing because you have to. As shown in the Book Battle content area examples, argument tactics were used to teach content and process—in a fun and engaging manner!

Sample Minilesson: Creating Credible Claims for Admirable Arguments (see Table 10.4)

One of the biggest concerns I hear from teachers is how to assist students in writing defensible and debatable claims. Hopefully, this minilesson will alleviate those worries!

Table 10.4 Argument writing minilesson

Unit/Genre: Argument writing
a. **Complete standard:** *Introduce claim(s) and organize the reasons and evidence clearly.* **Portion of the standard for emphasis in this lesson:** *Introduce claims.*

Modeling:
1. Share with students five claims that could be used to begin an argumentative paragraph on a single topic (Table 10.5). Ask students to evaluate the claims at face value—which one do they like best and why?
2. Introduce the definition of a claim to students (Table 10.3). Ask students to pay attention to the ideas of "debatable" and "defensible."
3. Begin an anchor chart for writing credible claims. Define "debatable" and "defensible" with students. Add "logical evidence and reasons are apparent" to the debatable and defensible.
4. Model taking a claim through the credibility process:
   a. Statement #1 is debatable because someone could state otherwise. Statement #1 is less defensible because the statement is pure opinion. Statement #1 could have evidence and reasons for it that would be hard to find.
   b. Model writing a new claim for Statement #1: Dogs are better than cats because dogs are naturally more sympathetic, as shown through several studies.

Guided Practice:
1. Ask students in pairs or small groups to choose another statement and take it through the steps of claim credibility—Is it debatable? Is it defensible? Can logical evidence and reasons be found to support it? If students find a claim lacking, they should rewrite it to strengthen its credibility.
2. Formative assessment: Have students share responses. Take note of students who struggle with this process. As a class, decide which claim would be the best to use to write an argument on this topic.

Directions for Independent Practice:
1. Ask students to examine an Everyday Writing piece for a claim. Have students take that claim through the claim credibility process. If they find their claim weak or lacking, they should rewrite the claim to strengthen it. Students can then continue to draft their argument writing piece.
2. If students finish early, direct them to begin a new essay/story, read independently, or revise or edit the current piece.

Reteaching ideas:
1. Work with students in small groups to revise existing claims using the credibility process.
2. Share with students more sample claims for revision.

Sharing ideas:
1. Students can work in pairs to evaluate each other's claims, using the Focused Question Card strategy.
2. As an exit slip, students could write their claims on a sticky note and stick it on the door on the way out. These could be collected and displayed to show ideas by other students.

Table 10.5   Five Claims on a Topic

Topic: Cats versus dogs
1. Dogs are better than cats because dogs are nicer.
2. Cats are better than dogs because cats have instincts that make them sympathetic to human emotions.
3. Dogs are better.
4. Cats are cooler and they feel soft.
5. Dogs and cats are equally good pets; it just depends on a person's preferences.

Common Core Connection

The strategies shared in the chapter fit well with the argument writing standards for both English/Language Arts teachers and Literacy Standards for Social Studies, Science, and Other Technical Subjects. The Book Battle Bracket matches well with the Speaking and Listening Standards (see Table 10.6).

Table 10.6   Writing Standards

Grade Level	4	5	6
Standard Addressed	**Writing** Write opinion pieces on topics or texts, supporting a point of view with reasons and information. Introduce a topic or text clearly, state an opinion, and create an organizational structure in which related ideas are grouped	**Writing** Write opinion pieces on topics or texts, supporting a point of view with reasons and information. Introduce a topic or text clearly, state an opinion, and create an organizational structure in which ideas are logically grouped	**Writing** Write arguments to support claims with clear reasons and relevant evidence. Introduce claim(s) and organize the reasons and evidence clearly. Support claim(s) with clear reasons and relevant

Grade Level	4	5	6
	to support the writer's purpose. Provide reasons that are supported by facts and details. Link opinion and reasons using words and phrases (e.g., *for instance, in order to, in addition*). Provide a concluding statement or section related to the opinion presented. **Speaking and Listening Standards** Report on a topic or text, tell a story, or recount an experience in an organized manner, using appropriate facts and relevant, descriptive details to support main ideas or themes; speak clearly at an understandable pace.	to support the writer's purpose. Provide logically ordered reasons that are supported by facts and details. Link opinion and reasons using words, phrases, and clauses (e.g., *consequently, specifically*). Provide a concluding statement or section related to the opinion presented. **Speaking and Listening Standards** Report on a topic or text or present an opinion, sequencing ideas logically and using appropriate facts and relevant, descriptive details to support main ideas or themes; speak clearly at an understandable pace.	evidence, using credible sources and demonstrating an understanding of the topic or text. Use words, phrases, and clauses to clarify the relationships among claim(s) and reasons. Establish and maintain a formal style. Provide a concluding statement or section that follows from the argument presented. **Speaking and Listening Standards** Present claims and findings, sequencing ideas logically and using pertinent descriptions, facts, and details to accentuate main ideas or themes; use appropriate eye contact, adequate volume, and clear pronunciation.

(Continued)

Table 10.6 Continued

	7	8	9–10
	Writing	**Writing**	**Writing**
	Write arguments to support claims with clear reasons and relevant evidence.	Write arguments to support claims with clear reasons and relevant evidence.	Write arguments to support claims in an analysis of substantive topics or texts, using valid reasoning and relevant and sufficient evidence.
	Introduce claim(s), acknowledge alternate or opposing claims, and organize the reasons and evidence logically.	Introduce claim(s), acknowledge and distinguish the claim(s) from alternate or opposing claims, and organize the reasons and evidence logically.	Introduce precise claim(s), distinguish the claim(s) from alternate or opposing claims, and create an organization that establishes clear relationships among claim(s), counterclaims, reasons, and evidence.
	Support claim(s) with logical reasoning and relevant evidence, using accurate, credible sources and demonstrating an understanding of the topic or text.	Support claim(s) with logical reasoning and relevant evidence, using accurate, credible sources and demonstrating an understanding of the topic or text.	Develop claim(s) and counterclaims fairly, supplying evidence for each while pointing out the strengths and limitations of both in a manner that anticipates the audience's knowledge level and concerns.
	Use words, phrases, and clauses to create cohesion and clarify the relationships among claim(s), reasons, and evidence.	Use words, phrases, and clauses to create cohesion and clarify the relationships among claim(s), counterclaims, reasons, and evidence.	
	Establish and maintain a formal style.	Establish and maintain a formal style.	
	Provide a concluding statement or		

	7	8	9–10
	section that follows from and supports the argument presented.	Provide a concluding statement or section that follows from and supports the argument presented.	Use words, phrases, and clauses to link the major sections of the text, create cohesion, and clarify the relationships between claim(s) and reasons, between reasons and evidence, and between claim(s) and counterclaims.
	Speaking and Listening Standards Present claims and findings, emphasizing salient points in a focused, coherent manner with pertinent descriptions, facts, details, and examples; use appropriate eye contact, adequate volume, and clear pronunciation.	**Speaking and Listening Standards** Present claims and findings, emphasizing salient points in a focused, coherent manner with relevant evidence, sound valid reasoning, and well-chosen details; use appropriate eye contact, adequate volume, and clear pronunciation.	Establish and maintain a formal style and objective tone while attending to the norms and conventions of the discipline in which they are writing. Provide a concluding statement or section that follows from and supports the argument presented.
			Speaking and Listening Standards Present information,

(*Continued*)

Table 10.6 Continued

	7	8	9–10
			findings, and supporting evidence clearly, concisely, and logically such that listeners can follow the line of reasoning and the organization, development, substance, and style are appropriate to purpose, audience, and task.

Literacy Standards for History/Social Studies, Science, and Other Technical Subjects

	6–8	9–10

	Writing
	Write arguments focused on *discipline-specific content.*
	    Introduce claim(s) about a topic or issue, acknowledge and distinguish the claim(s) from alternate or opposing claims, and organize the reasons and evidence logically.
	    Support claim(s) with logical reasoning
		Writing
		Write arguments focused on *discipline-specific content.*
		    Introduce precise claim(s), distinguish the claim(s) from alternate or opposing claims, and create an organization that establishes clear relationships among the claim(s), counterclaims, reasons, and evidence.

	6–8	9–10
	and relevant, accurate data and evidence that demonstrate an understanding of the topic or text, using credible sources. Use words, phrases, and clauses to create cohesion and clarify the relationships among claim(s), counterclaims, reasons, and evidence. Establish and maintain a formal style. Provide a concluding statement or section that follows from and supports the argument presented.	Develop claim(s) and counterclaims fairly, supplying data and evidence for each while pointing out the strengths and limitations of both claim(s) and counterclaims in a discipline-appropriate form and in a manner that anticipates the audience's knowledge level and concerns. Use words, phrases, and clauses to link the major sections of the text, create cohesion, and clarify the relationships between claim(s) and reasons, between reasons and evidence, and between claim(s) and counterclaims. Establish and maintain a formal style and objective tone while attending to the norms and conventions of the discipline in which they are writing. Provide a concluding statement or section that follows from or supports the argument presented.

Action Steps

Writing arguments can be a great way to engage students in content. It's time to take some action . . .

1. Go to "Room for Debate" on the *New York Times* website (www.nytimes.com/roomfordebate). Identify at least two articles on a single topic that you can use to teach the CREW strategy in your classroom.
   a. Article #1:

   _____

   _____

   b. Article #2:

   _____

   _____

2. How could you see using the Book Battle Bracket in your classroom? Would students debate the merits of books? A topic? Events? Historical figures? Think about the best way to use this engaging strategy in your classroom.

   _____

   _____

Works Cited

Andrews, R., Torgeson, C., Low, G., & McGuinn, N. (2009). Teaching argument writing to 7–14 year olds: An international review of the evidence of successful practice. *Cambridge Journal of Education, 39*, 291–310.

Chapman, T., Hobbel, N., & Alvarado, N. (2011). Real-time teaching. *Journal of Adolescent and Adult Literacy, 54*, 539–541.

Dean, D. (2006). *Strategic writing: The writing process and beyond in the secondary English classroom.* Urbana, IL: NCTE.

Hillocks, G. (2011). *Teaching argument writing, grades 6–12.* Portsmouth, NH: Heinemann.

Moore, N., & MacArthur, C. (2011). The effects of being a reader and of observing readers on fifth-grade students' argumentative writing and revising. *Reading and Writing: An Interdisciplinary Journal, 25*, 1449–1478.

Sampson, V., Enderle, P., Grooms, J., & Witte, S. (2013). Writing to learn by learning to write during the school science laboratory: Helping middle and high school students develop argumentative writing skills as they learn core ideas. *Science Education, 97*, 643–670.

Santa, C., Havens, L., & Valdes, B. (2004). *Project CRISS: Creating independence through student-owned strategies.* Dubuque, IA: Kendall Hunt.

Toulmin, S. (1958). *The use of argument.* Cambridge: Cambridge University Press.

Warren, J. (2010). Taming the warrant in Toulmin's model of argument. *English Journal, 99*, 41–46.

Wilfong, L. (2014). *Nonfiction strategies that work: Do this—not that!* New York: Routledge.

Template 10.1   RAFT Graphic Organizer

Name: _____

Date: _____

Role	Audience	Format	Topic

Template 10.2 CREW Collector Sheet

Name: _____

Date: _____

Text 1 Title:	Text 2 Title:
Claim: _____ _____ _____ _____	Claim: _____ _____ _____ _____
Reason: 1. _____ _____ 2. _____ _____ 3. _____ _____ _____	Reason: 1. _____ _____ 2. _____ _____ 3. _____ _____ _____
Evidence: 1. _____ _____ 2. _____ _____ 3. _____ _____ _____	Evidence: 1. _____ _____ 2. _____ _____ 3. _____ _____ _____
Warrant: _____ _____ _____	Warrant: _____ _____ _____

Template 10.3   Book Battle Bracket

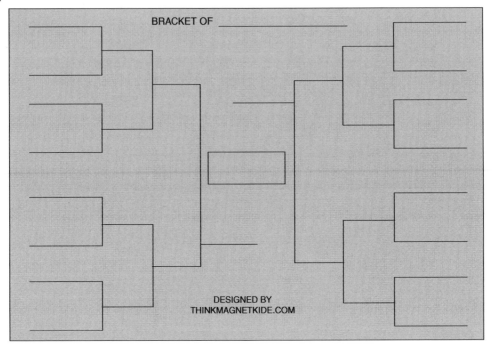

BRACKET OF _____

DESIGNED BY
THINKMAGNETKIDE.COM

© 2015, *Writing Strategies That Work,* Lori G. Wilfong, Routledge